TRUTH ON ITS HEAD

TRUTH ON ITS HEAD

Unusual Wisdom in the Paradoxes of the Bible

Warren W. Wiersbe

WEAVER BOOK
COMPANY

WOOSTER, OHIO

Truth on Its Head: Unusual Wisdom in the Paradoxes of the Bible
© 2016 by Warren W. Wiersbe

Published by
Weaver Book Company
1190 Summerset Dr.
Wooster, OH 44691
weaverbookcompany.com

Cover design: Frank Gutbrod
Interior design: {In a Word}
Editorial: Line for Line Publishing Services

Print ISBN: 978-1-941337-57-8
EPUB ISBN: 978-1-941337-63-9

Library of Congress Cataloging-in-Publication Data

Names: Wiersbe, Warren W., author.
Title: Truth on its head : unusual wisdom in the paradoxes of the Bible /
Warren W. Wiersbe.
Description: Wooster : Weaver Book Company, 2016.
Identifiers: LCCN 2016003049 | ISBN 9781941337578
Subjects: LCSH: Bible — Language, style. | Paradox in the Bible. |
Bible — Criticism, interpretation, etc.
Classification: LCC BS537 .W544 2016 | DDC 220.6 — dc23
LC record available at http://lccn.loc.gov/2016003049

Printed in the United States of America
16 17 18 19 20 / 5 4 3 2 1

Contents

Prologue:
Contradiction Becomes Illumination

A paradox is a statement that attracts attention because it seems to be contradictory. This arouses curiosity and we are puzzled. But as we meditate on the statement, we go deeper into some important facet of life and learn something new. Paradoxes are marvelous instructors.

"Nothing succeeds like success" is a familiar saying, but what about "There is nothing that fails like success"? I read that statement in the first chapter of G. K. Chesterton's *Heretics*. Chesterton used a paradox to get my attention and arouse my curiosity. Hillel, the famous first-century rabbi wrote, "My lowliness is my loftiness; my loftiness is my lowliness." It sounds a great deal like our Lord's, "For whoever exalts himself will be humbled, and he who humbles himself will be exalted" (Luke 14:11).

Our heavenly Father wants all of His children to make progress in the Christian life, and every true Christian should want to obey Him and mature. The apostle Peter admonished his readers to "grow in the grace and knowledge of our Lord and Savior Jesus Christ" (2 Peter 3:18). If we want to glorify our Lord, we must grow. According to the apostle John, God's family is made up of "little children . . . fathers . . . and young men" (1 John 2:12–14). And while all believers are "little children" of God, we must heed the admonition of Hebrews 5:12–14 and grow from childhood into spiritual adulthood. No more baby food! Solid food is the diet for the maturing saints. Jesus wants us to move from "fruit" to "more fruit" to "much fruit" (John 15:1–8). Why? "By this My Father is glorified" (v. 8). We can make progress in the Christian life only if we do the following:

- obey God's precepts,
- believe and claim God's promises,
- understand God's principles, and
- enter into the depths of God's paradoxes.

Precepts are the commands and instructions the Father gives us and which we must obey if we want to please Him and enjoy His blessings. Promises are the encouragements the Father shares with His children to assure them that He will see them through as they trust and obey. Both the precepts and the promises are based on the principles found in the character and purposes of the Lord. Because God is holy, He wants us to be holy (Lev. 19:2; 20:7; 1 Peter 1:15–16); and if we walk in obedience, He will bless us and make us a blessing.

The word "paradox" may not be as familiar to you as "precepts," "promises," and "principles," but it is just as important. Paradoxes share truths that help us go deeper into the truth of God's word. The Scottish preacher George H. Morrison said, "For man does not live by reconciling mysteries; he lives by mysteries he cannot reconcile."[1] If you will scan the table of contents, you will see what I mean. How do we get strength out of weakness? Honor from humility? And progress out of standing still? All of these are par-

---

1   George H. Morrison, *The Weaving of Glory* (London: Hodder and Stoughton, 1913), 245.

adoxes — *and they work!* Inspired by the Holy Spirit, Paul wrote a string of paradoxes in 2 Corinthians 6:9–10: . . . as unknown, and yet well-known; as dying, and behold we live;

> as chastened, and yet not killed;
> as sorrowful, yet always rejoicing;
> as poor, yet making many rich;
> as having nothing, and yet possessing all things.

When the believers in Corinth heard these words read to their church gathering, it must have awakened them and aroused their attention. "How can we die and live at the same time, or sorrow and always rejoice?" they would ask. "If I am poor, how can I make others rich? If I have nothing, how can I claim to possess everything?" Paradoxes attract our attention, challenge our faith and provoke us into thinking deeper and asking wiser questions. They lead us into truths that, if we act upon them, will help us to grow out of spiritual childhood and into the blessings of spiritual maturity. The well-known philosopher Alfred North Whitehead wrote, "A clash of doctrines is not a disaster — it is an opportunity."[2] For the Christian, a seeming contradiction in a paradox is a challenge to grow. What an opportunity!

In my reading of literature, old and new, I frequently encounter paradoxes. On December 5, 1856, the American naturalist Henry David Thoreau wrote in his journal, "It is the greatest of all advantages to enjoy no advantage at all. I find it invariably true, the poorer I am, the richer I am." George Orwell put a clever (and quotable) paradox into chapter 10 of his popular novel *Animal Farm*: "All animals are equal, but some animals are more equal

---

2   Alfred North Whitehead, *Science and the Modern World* (New York: Macmillan, 1929), 266.

than others." In a newspaper interview, a young Hollywood actress said, "Deep down, I'm pretty superficial." The American essayist Ralph Waldo Emerson wrote, "God hides things by putting them near us."

Even television makes its contribution. After reporting on the war in Vietnam, the popular news analyst Edward R. Murrow said, "Anyone who isn't confused really doesn't understand the situation." Finally, a learned theologian said, "We are all free to do as we must."

In the chapters that follow, I deal with fifteen biblical paradoxes and try to show what they mean and how they can help us mature spiritually in every area of life. The paradoxes are arranged in no special order and you may want to begin with those that interest you the most. But be sure to keep your Bible near at hand so you can look up and read the verses I cite but do not quote. Each citation is important, so please do not ignore them.

The title of this book originated with the British essayist G. K. Chesterton who defined a paradox as "truth standing on its head to gain attention."

1

The Joyful Fear of the Lord

Specific sense of Respect
Submission
God Phobia or Theophobia

Serve the LORD with fear, and rejoice with trembling. (Ps. 2:11)

You who fear the LORD, praise Him! All you descendants of Jacob, glorify Him, and fear Him, all you offspring of Israel! (Ps. 22:23)

He will bless those who fear the LORD, both small and great. (Ps. 115:13)

For as the heavens are high above the earth, so great is His mercy toward those who fear Him. . . . As a father pities his children, so the LORD pities those who fear Him. (Ps. 103:11, 13)

Blessed is the man who fears the LORD. (Ps. 112:1)

Blessed is everyone who fears the LORD, who walks in His ways. (Ps. 128:1)

The fear of the LORD is the beginning of wisdom, and the knowledge of the Holy One is understanding. (Prov. 9:10)

The fear of the LORD leads to life, and he who has it will abide in satisfaction; he will not be visited with evil. (Prov. 19:23)

His delight is in the fear of the LORD. (Isa. 11:3)

His mercy is on those who fear Him. (Luke 1:50)

WHEN WE WERE YOUNG BELIEVERS, we exulted in the joy of the Lord. After all, our sins were forgiven, we were learning from the Scriptures, and the Holy Spirit was enabling us to walk in victory. We were certain that this exciting new life would never change — but it did!

If our faith is to grow and become stronger, it must be tested; and so temptations and trials confront us as the world, the flesh, and the devil oppose us (Eph. 2:1–3; 1 John 2:15–17). Occasionally we lose the victory and deliberately disobey the Lord. Then we confessed our sins, and from our hearts prayed, "Restore to me the joy of Your salvation" (Ps. 51:12). We claimed 1 John 1:9 and got up and made a new beginning.

But the enemy doesn't want us to be joyful so he begins to accuse us (Zech. 3:1–5; Rev. 12:10). He wants the memory of our sins to trouble us, discourage us, and make us worry about consequences. When Satan tempted us, he whispered, "Don't worry, you can get away with this!" But after we sinned, he shouted, "You will *never* get away with this!" Then the fear of the Lord moved in and we began to wonder if the Father would chasten us. The joy of the Lord and the fear of the Lord must be replaced by *the joyful fear of the Lord.*

Let's think about what it means to experience joyful fear continually instead of riding the rollercoaster of joy and fear — up one day and down the next.

The Joy of the Lord

Jesus was a man of sorrows (Isa. 53:3), but He was also a man of joy (John 15:11). I mentioned this in a message at a summer Bible conference some years ago, and after the meeting an elderly woman confronted me and scolded me soundly for that statement. She was certain that Jesus was not joyful and that I was twisting the Scriptures. I showed her John 15:11 and 16:20–24, plus Luke 10:17–24. "If Jesus had no joy, how could He give it to His disciples and to us?" She turned on her heels and marched away in anger, upset with my ignorance. If ever a believer needed joy, she was the one!

As God's beloved children, we are blessed with the joy of the Lord and do not depend on the happiness of this world. Happiness depends primarily on happenings. If our circumstances are going well, we are happy; if they fall apart, we are unhappy and we complain. The joy of the Lord is something quite different from mere happiness. Unsaved people may experience happiness, but only true believers in Jesus Christ may have this deeper and more satisfying joy of the Lord (Luke 1:46; Phil. 3:1; 4:4, 10). The joy of the Lord depends on the Holy Spirit within us and not on what is happening around us. It is the work of the Holy Spirit to grow within us the fruit of the Spirit, which includes joy (Gal. 5:22). It is a joy produced by the Father, for "the joy of the LORD is your strength" (Neh. 8:10). Our joy is given by the Son (John 15:11; 16:20–24) and nourished by the Spirit (1 Thess. 1:6; Gal. 5:22).

The joy of the Lord is beautifully illustrated in the three so-called lost parables in Luke 15. The shepherd rejoiced that he found his lost sheep, the woman that she found her lost coin, and the father that his lost son returned home — and they shared their joy with others. Even the angels in heaven rejoice when a lost sinner is saved (Luke 15:7, 10)! Should we not also rejoice because we have a Shepherd who cares for us and a Father who loves us, forgives us, and spreads a feast for us? Paul wrote from prison, "Rejoice in the Lord always. Again I will say, rejoice" (Phil. 4:4; see 3:1; 4:10). Peter describes our joy as being "inexpressible and full of glory" (1 Peter 1:8). We experience it but we can't always explain it! "In Your presence is fullness of joy," wrote David (Ps.

16:11); and an anonymous psalmist rejoiced because God reigns from His heavenly throne (Ps. 67:3–4).

Besides our own salvation and the joy of leading others to Christ, we have so many good causes for rejoicing! We "rejoice in hope of the glory of God" (Rom. 5:1–2; see 12:12) and in the blessings of the word of God (Pss. 19:8; 119:14, 92, 111, 162). "Your words were found, and I ate them, and Your word was to me the joy and rejoicing of my heart, for I am called by Your name, O LORD God of hosts" (Jer. 15:16). Whenever I have been in painful circumstances, the promises of God have encouraged me and given me joy — and they did the Thessalonian believers (1 Thess. 1:6). Whenever we sow the seed of the word of God, we have God's promise of one day rejoicing at the harvest (Ps. 126:5–6); and think of the joy of answered prayer (John 16:24)! Our hearts ought to be filled with joyful praise all day long (Pss. 33:1–5; 98:4–6)! Jesus wants His joy to be fulfilled in our lives (John 17:13), and it will be if we live for all that rejoices Him.

In chapter 17 of his *Letters to Malcolm*, C. S. Lewis defines joy as "the serious business of heaven." Sin ultimately brings sorrow and regret, which is one reason why Jesus died for sinners. Faith in Jesus Christ not only gives us the forgiveness of our sins but also the joys of knowing God's will, the power to obey His will, and the reward of knowing we are pleasing the sovereign God. All that the Father and Son and Spirit have said and done has but one goal: that we might possess eternal life and abundant life and rejoice in doing God's will. Lewis was right: joy is "the serious business of heaven." Is that the "business" we are in?

The Fear of the Lord

The fear of the Lord is that reverent respect for God that is born, not of terror, but of knowledge, love, and faith. The better we

4

know God, the more we love and trust Him and the more we want to please Him. In the spiritual life, joy without fear can be shallow and careless, while fear without joy can be destructive. Terror paralyzes us but godly fear energizes us. Mingled with joy, godly fear is a great source of power. "Therefore, since we are receiving a kingdom which cannot be shaken, let us have grace, by which we may serve God acceptably and with reverent and godly fear. For our God is a consuming fire" (Heb. 12:28–29). Without a proper fear of the Lord, how can we serve Him acceptably?

I learned very early in life that my parents and my teachers meant business when they issued orders and that my job was to listen and obey. If I rebelled, I might be disciplined, but even worse, I would have missed an opportunity to learn and make progress in maturing. Respect for authority opens the doors to effective learning and living. The phrases "the fear of the Lord" and "the fear of God" are used more than one hundred times in Scripture. The believers in the early church walked in the fear of the Lord, and so should we — and be happy about it (Acts 9:31; Heb. 12:28–29). In one sense, the phrase "the fear of the Lord" is equivalent to "faith in the Lord." After the people of Israel crossed the Red Sea, fear became faith and faith turned into joy. "Thus Israel saw the great work which the LORD had done in Egypt, so the people feared the LORD, and believed the LORD and His servant Moses" (Exod. 14:31). After that, Israel burst out into joyful song and praised the Lord (Exod. 15).

If there is one thing needed in our churches today it is reverence for the sovereign Lord, a holy awe, a genuine fear of God. When Israel came to Mount Sinai, God demonstrated His majesty and His glory, and Moses and the people trembled (Exod. 19). Just as children must learn to respect their parents, students their teachers, and military men and women their officers, so God's children must learn to respect and honor God *so they might grow into the love of God!* After Paul listed the godless activities of the sinful world (Rom. 3:10–17), he explained why men and women live that way: "There is no fear of God before their eyes" (v. 18). David started Psalm 36 with that statement and Paul quoted it.

There is no fear of judgment that makes people run and hide, as Adam and Eve did after they sinned (Gen. 3:10). There is no fear of the unknown such as the people of Israel experienced at Mount Sinai (Exod. 19). In our world of scientific wonders, we think we know everything and can control everything; and then hurricanes and tornadoes come and we head for a hiding place and start to pray. As the saying goes, we can run but we cannot hide! "Fear God and keep His commandments, for this is the whole duty of man" (Eccl. 12:13, KJV). But the fear of the child of God is not so much "Will He hurt me?" as "Am I going to grieve Him and hinder His work?" Our disobedience grieves the Holy Spirit (Eph. 4:30), just as the stubborn disobedience of children wounds the loving hearts of their parents. It is a joyful experience in the life of a family when the children start asking themselves, "Will this hurt others?" instead of "Will others hurt me?"

"The fear of the LORD is the beginning of wisdom, and the knowledge of the Holy One is understanding" (Prov. 9:10). *Knowing and respecting the instructors is as important as knowing and receiving the lessons they teach.* Knowledge deals primarily with people, places, things, facts, and events; but wisdom pulls it all together and reveals values, principles, and truths. It is important to know the who, what, when, and where of life; but we also need to know the why and the how. Wisdom is the correct use of knowledge for the building of character and a successful life. I have a coffee mug with the statement "Reputation can be made in a moment. Character takes a lifetime." Let me amend it: "Character takes a lifetime of experience, knowledge, and wisdom." Providing we know the Lord and trust Him, a lifetime of experience and

DEPART FROM EVIL OR WICKEDNESS
REMAIN SINLESS AS A Child of God.

knowledge will produce wisdom and character. We can be smart and repeatedly do dumb things, but if we have wisdom, we will do the right things.

God blesses and uses those who understand the fear of the Lord, for it is "by the fear of the LORD [that] one departs from evil" (Prov. 16:6). "The fear of the LORD leads to life, and he who has it will abide in satisfaction; he will not be visited with evil" (Prov. 19:23). "The secret of the LORD is with those who fear Him, and He will show them His covenant" (Ps. 25:14). Psalm 112 states some of the blessings the person will receive who "fears the LORD, who delights greatly in His commandments" (v. 1). I heard the late Dr. V. Raymond Edman, former president of Wheaton (IL) College, expound this psalm. He called the fear of the Lord "the fear that casts out every other fear," and he is right! Read the psalm for yourself and you will agree.

The Joyful Fear of the Lord

Thanks to paradox, reverent fear and joyful blessing can be friends and work together to make each believer a maturing and faithful child of God. In Scripture we often find joy and fear cooperating. Psalm 95 begins with rejoicing (vv. 1–5) and ends with worship and the fear of God (vv. 6–11). And Isaiah 11:3 says, "His delight is in the fear of the LORD." In his letter to the church at Philippi, Paul mentions joy at least eighteen times, and yet he commands the believers to "work out your own salvation with fear and trembling" (2:12). He himself rejoices and yet weeps over the carelessness of some believers (3:18).

How do God's people properly balance the fear of the Lord with the joy of the Lord? We must know the word of God and trust it and we must yield to the Holy Spirit and allow Him to fill us and work in our lives. The Scriptures are rich with narratives about

God's people who experienced joyful fear of the Lord, beginning with Abraham's offering of his son Isaac (Gen. 22; Heb. 11:17–19) and closing with the book of Revelation, where twenty-six times you find Jesus the Lamb but also Jesus the Lion (5:6; 6:16–17). The Lamb died for our sins, but those who oppose Him discover that the Lamb is also the Lion who punishes rebellious sinners.

Our Lord Himself demonstrates the balance between the joy of the Lord and the fear of the Lord. At the transfiguration, Jesus was radiant with heavenly glory while discussing with Moses and Elijah His approaching death on the cross (Luke 9:30–31). Jesus suffered greatly on the cross, yet by faith He laid hold of "the joy that was set before Him" (Heb. 12:2; see Jude 24). Psalm 22, the psalm of the crucifixion, unites fear and praise (vv. 22–26). The balance between suffering and glory is one of the major themes of Peter's first epistle. Peter taught that the church of Jesus Christ in his day was heading toward severe opposition and official persecution, and he told the saints how to be ready. If we are not prepared for the fiery trial of 1 Peter 4:12–19, how can we experience the joy Jesus describes in Matthew 5:11–12? I believe the church needs this message today.

Our Lord's disciples also demonstrate the balance between the joy and fear of the Lord. When you read the book of Acts, you learn how the early Christians overcame persecution to the glory of God. Their first aim in life was to magnify Jesus Christ and proclaim the gospel (Acts 4:20). If their ministries brought them beatings, imprisonments, and even martyrdom, they accepted God's will and sought to glorify Him (Acts 4:1–22). Daily they devoted themselves to the word of God and prayer (Acts 6:4), and they depended on the fullness of the Spirit for the power and wisdom they needed. They took their stand boldly for the truth of God (Acts 4:21–31). But I fear our "business as usual" ministries today, and the absence of prayer and coura-

MAAR tR dm
(suffering of death) 8

geous witnessing, all mitigate against overcoming the enemy and reaching the lost. We are not prepared for the fire (1 Peter 4:12). The German martyr Dietrich Bonhoeffer defined a Christian as "someone who shares the sufferings of God in this world." Does that describe us?

Joyful fear is certainly a paradox but not an impossibility. Blessed are the balanced!

MAAR Fe

When We Are Weak,
We Can Be Strong

> And lest I should be exalted above measure by the abundance of the revelations, a thorn in the flesh was given to me, a messenger of Satan to buffet me, lest I be exalted above measure. Concerning this thing, I pleaded with the Lord three times that it might depart from me. And He said to me, "My grace is sufficient for you, for My strength is made perfect in weakness." Therefore most gladly I will rather boast in my infirmities, that the power of Christ may rest upon me. Therefore I take pleasure in infirmities, in reproaches, in needs, in persecutions, in distresses, for Christ's sake. For when I am weak, then I am strong. (2 Cor. 12:7–10)

SOMEONE HAS DEFINED A SECRET as something you repeat to one person at a time. That definition may apply to some people but not to the apostle Paul. He kept a secret hidden in his heart for fourteen years (2 Cor. 12:1–4), and the only reason he finally shared it was to defend his ministry. He was being attacked by troublemakers in the church at Corinth, people who questioned his apostolic authority. Paul had gone to heaven and come back and had never told anybody about it! To keep Paul from getting proud of these remarkable experiences, the Lord gave him "a thorn in the flesh." Nobody knows what this thorn was — and it's futile to speculate. The important thing is to know how God dealt with Paul because this is the way He might want to deal with us.

Unexpected Problems (2 Cor. 12:7)

A friend who had ministered in China told me about a Chinese Christian who was made an elder in one of the churches. When the pastor was in town, this elder was a great help; but when the pastor would go on evangelistic trips, the elder's personality would change radically and he would create serious problems in the church. When the pastor returned, the elder returned to normal. The man finally confessed the sin that was wrecking his life and his church — pride. "When I was ordained," the elder said, "Satan whispered in my ear, 'Now you are somebody important,' and I believed him. Pride got hold of me and I stopped being a minister and became a menace." God delivered the man and he set about repairing the damage he had done.

At his conversion, Paul had seen Jesus in glory and heard Him speak (Acts 9:1–9), and Paul's visit to heaven was an even more extraordinary experience. Like any believer, he could have become proud, but the Lord prevented him from boasting. There are times when the Lord must chasten us because of past sin (Heb. 12: 3–11), but there are also times when God disciplines us *to prevent future sin.* I have wondered at times why God permitted certain painful events to occur in my life, but I will understand it fully when I get to heaven. Paul knew why God gave him his thorn in the flesh: "lest I should be exalted above measure" (2 Cor. 12:7). Note that Paul repeats the statement. He got the message!

After a certain amount of success in life, it's very easy for us to become proud and confident of our own abilities. King Uzziah of Judah was greatly helped by the Lord and "his fame spread far and wide. . . . But when he was strong his heart was lifted up, to his destruction" (2 Chron. 26:15–16). "Pride goes before destruction, and a haughty spirit before a fall" (Prov. 16:18). God still had work for Paul to do, so He sent a thorn to humble him, and it worked! *Strength that knows itself to be strength becomes weakness, but weakness that knows itself to be weakness becomes strength.*

A similar experience almost kept young Joseph from enjoying God's best in his life. He was a godly young man, intelligent and in touch with the Lord; but he did not know how to handle the truths God was sharing with him (Gen. 37, 39). He was in danger of getting proud. The Lord sent Joseph to Egypt as a slave and there he was very successful, but then the Lord put him into prison to suffer and be equipped to serve as the second ruler in the land. "Humble yourselves in the sight of the Lord, and He will lift you up" (James 4:10). If we accept the unexpected difficulties of life that God sends us, we will go from weakness to strength and glorify His name; but if we depend on our own wisdom and abilities and want our own way, we will only grow weaker. Strength that knows it is strength will become weakness, but weakness that knows it is weakness will become strength *if we wholly trust the Lord.* When Paul first went to minister in Corinth, he was overwhelmed with weakness and fear and trembling. His preaching was not like the oratory of the popular pagan teachers in Corinth, but simple and compassionate. He did not want the people to be impressed with *him* but with Jesus and trust in Him (see 1 Cor. 2:1–5). He told the believers to follow Christ and imitate Him. Paul was not a celebrity; he was a servant of Jesus Christ.

Our heavenly Father knows how to balance our lives so that success will not exalt us or pain and failure defeat us. Jesus was "crucified in weakness, yet He lives by the power of God" (2 Cor. 13:4). We can glory in the cross because Jesus turned its seeming weakness and defeat into power and victory (1 Cor. 1:18–2:8; Col. 2:15; Gal. 6:14). A man of many trials and infirmities, Paul identified with Christ's suffering and it released power into his life. We cannot explain it but we can experience it. Paul knew he had not yet attained perfection in the Christian life so he kept pressing on (Phil. 3:12). Whenever I get the foolish idea that I have arrived, my Father reminds me that I still have a long way to go. And His reminders are difficult to ignore! (My computer often humbles me.) When I admit my feebleness, then God manifests His strength.

We never know when unexpected pains and problems will appear on the scene or what blessings the Father has in store for us. We walk by faith, not by sight, and we can be sure the Father will not abandon us.

Unanswered Prayers (2 Cor. 12:8)

It must have disturbed Paul when the Lord did not answer his prayers, because Paul was a man of faith who knew how to pray in God's will (Rom. 8:26–28). When the Lord instructed Ananias to go to Paul and baptize him and restore his sight, He added, "for behold, he is praying" (Acts 9:11). Prior to that time, Paul had been preying upon God's people, but now he was praying to the Lord and waiting for further orders.

Paul began his Christian life in prayer and to the very end it continued in prayer. Like Jesus in Gethsemane, Paul prayed three times that his cup of suffering might be taken from him, and like Jesus (Mark 14:35–41), he accepted God's will. In his excellent commentary on 1 John, Robert Law writes, "The purpose of prayer is not to get man's will done in heaven but to get God's will done on earth." While on their pilgrimage to the Promised Land, the nation of Israel begged the Lord to give them meat to eat. "He gave them their request, but sent leanness into their soul" (Ps. 106:15; Num. 11). In other words, the people got their answer *but they lost the blessing.* God did not answer Paul's request and remove

the thorn, but He did meet Paul's needs and give him the blessing
that would enable him to continue his ministry.

Paul was a man of prayer who encouraged others to pray, and
he was not ashamed to ask his Christian friends to pray for him
(Rom. 15:30–32; 2 Cor. 1:8–11; Eph. 6:19–20; Phil. 1:19; 1 Thess. 5:25;
2 Thess. 3:1–2). I have often meditated on Paul's prayers found in
his epistles, and this has strengthened my own prayer life. Paul
prayed without ceasing (Rom. 1:9; 1 Thess. 1:3; 2:13; 5:17; 2 Tim.
1:3), and it made no difference where he was — in a private home
(Acts 9:11), in the temple (Acts 22:17), with local church leaders
(Acts 13:1–3; 20:36–38; 21:5), in prison (Acts 16:25), or aboard a
ship in a storm (Acts 27:35). Perhaps he patterned his prayer life
after David and Daniel, who also prayed in a special way three
times a day (Ps. 55:17; Dan. 6:10).

It was perfectly natural for Paul to ask God to remove the
thorn. When we face problems or feel pain, it's normal to seek
God's help, for the Lord commands us to cast all our cares upon
Him (1 Peter 5:7). But it is also a good thing to come to the place
where we are grateful for *unanswered* prayer. For example, Moses
forfeited entering the Promised Land because he had disobeyed
the Lord (Num. 20:1–13). He prayed several times for the Lord to
change His mind, but God refused. But centuries later the Lord
gave Moses an even better blessing when He permitted him and
Elijah to have glorious fellowship with Jesus on the Mount of
Transfiguration (Matt. 17:1–13). That was a postponed blessing
worth waiting for!

Unanswered prayer might mean that we have hidden sins in
our lives that need to be confessed and forsaken (Ps. 66:18), or
that we are not praying in the will of God. "Now this is the confidence that we have in Him, that if we ask anything according to
His will, He hears us. And if we know that He hears us, whatever
we ask, we know that we have the petitions that we have asked

of Him" (1 John 5:14–15). James 4:15 instructs us to pray, "If the Lord wills . . ." We discover the will of God as we wait before Him, worship Him, search the Scriptures, and tell Him we are willing to do His will (John 7:17). I am not smart enough to tell my Father what He should do and when He should do it, but I think I am smart enough to submit to Him and say, "Your will be done" (see Luke 22:42).

Unlimited Power (2 Cor. 12:9)

The Lord did not remove Paul's thorn in the flesh, but He did give him the grace he needed to turn the burden into a blessing. By His grace, the Lord transformed weakness into strength. This does not mean that Paul was now able to *endure* the pain but that he was able to *enlist* the pain and make it work *for* him and not *against* him. "My grace is sufficient for you," the Lord told Paul, "for My strength is made perfect in weakness" (2 Cor. 12:9). The word "grace" is used sixteen times in 2 Corinthians. Someone has made an acronym out of the word GRACE:

> God's
> Resources
> Available to
> Christians
> Everywhere

God's grace is God's love in action, meeting every need and using every circumstance to edify us and to glorify Jesus. The Lord does not measure our inability but He tests our availability so He can give us His divine ability. "Now thanks be to God who always leads us in triumph in Christ" (2 Cor. 2:14).

In 2 Corinthians 2, the words "sufficient" and "sufficiency" are important. After describing the so-called Roman triumph parade (vv. 12–16), Paul asks the question, "And who is sufficient for these things?" Who is sufficient to share in Christ's glorious victory? Who is sufficient to stand between life and death as we share the gospel with the lost? Paul answers the question in 2 Corinthians 3:5: "Not that we are sufficient of ourselves to think of anything as being from ourselves, but our sufficiency is from God, who also made us sufficient and ministers of the new covenant." Christ's victory guarantees our sufficiency, if we trust Him and seek only to glorify Him. Christ is sufficient for all our *spiritual* needs (2 Cor. 3:5–6).

According to 2 Corinthians 9:8, Christ is also sufficient for all our *material* needs. "And God is able to make all grace abound toward you, that you, always having all sufficiency in all things, have an abundance for every good work." Paul was taking up a "love offering" for the suffering Jewish believers in the Holy Land, and he was encouraging the Corinthian believers to fulfill their promises and make their contribution. The money we give to the Lord to minister to the needs of believers and to evangelize unbelievers is an investment in eternal blessing. (I will go into greater detail in the following chapter.) During our years of ministry, my wife and I have seen the Lord multiply gifts in wonderful ways and meet our needs as well as the needs of those whom we help to support.

Besides the spiritual and the material, there is a third area of sufficiency — the physical. As we have learned from 2 Corinthians 12, Paul had a physical problem that was painful, and in spite of Paul's fervent prayers, it was permanent. We would know nothing about this matter had Paul not written about it to the saints in Corinth. But the God who met the spiritual and financial needs also met Paul's physical needs! "My grace is sufficient for you, for My strength is made perfect in weakness" (2 Cor. 12:9).

Our care of the physical body is as much a spiritual discipline as using our time wisely and spending our money wisely. The Christian's body is not only God's temple (1 Cor. 6:19–20) but also God's tool for accomplishing His work on earth (Rom. 6:13; 12:1–2). The proper use of food, exercise, rest, and hygiene is as much a spiritual discipline as our use of time, money, and ministry opportunities. As we get older, we must learn to adjust our schedules, activities, and diets so that we conserve our strength and make good use of our opportunities. God's weakness is stronger than our strength (1 Cor. 1:25), and if we trust His grace, He will see us through. "And of His fullness we have all received, and grace for grace" (John 1:16).

As you read your Bible, you meet men and women who did extraordinary things for the Lord because they had no confidence in the flesh (Phil. 3:3) or in other people (Ps. 118:8). They depended only on the grace of God and He turned their weakness into strength (Heb. 11:34). "Some trust in chariots, and some in horses, but we will remember the name of the LORD our God" (Ps. 20:7). When God calls and commands us, He always graciously provides all that we need so we can obey and serve Him. Paul boasted about his weakness because it glorified the Lord who turned that weakness into power (2 Cor. 12:9). When we are willing to be nothing in ourselves and let God get the glory, He is willing to meet every need, solve every problem, and defeat every enemy — in His own way and His own time.

There are two words in the Greek language for the word "another." One means "another of the same kind" (*allos*), and the second means "another of a different kind" (*heteros*). When Jesus spoke to His disciples about "another Helper" (John 14:15–18), the word in the Greek text is *allos*, "another of the same kind." He was saying that the Holy Spirit is a Helper to us today *just as Jesus was to His disciples!* The same Holy Spirit who taught and empowered Peter and the other disciples is available to minister to us today, if we will permit Him. For us to disobey the Spirit and do things our own way is to grieve Him and lose the guidance and power we so desperately need.

But I must add this: we also need the Spirit to help us sit still and wait. "But those who wait on the LORD shall renew their strength; they shall mount up with wings as eagles, they shall run and not be weary, they shall walk and not faint" (Isa. 40:31). "In quietness and confidence shall be your strength" (Isa. 30:15). In many churches, instead of quietness and confidence, we have noise and nervousness, and the Lord is not glorified. I have known believers who wearied themselves by running from conference to conference and meeting to meeting without taking time to rest and meditate, as Jesus commanded His disciples (Mark 6:31). Unlimited power is available to us as we wait on the Lord and trust Him, for His grace is always sufficient and efficient. As we wait before the Lord, He is at work on our behalf because all things are working together for our good and His glory.

Unbelievable Pleasure (2 Cor. 12:10)

How can people take pleasure in pain? Do they suffer from some kind of mental or emotional affliction? Paul was certainly not unbalanced, nor does he want us to be unbalanced. We must pay close attention to the context. Paul could rejoice in his sufferings because they were for the sake of Jesus, his Savior and Lord. Any suffering we bear for Him is nothing compared to all that He has suffered for us. Paul was not concerned about what the people thought but what Jesus thought. This was "the fellowship of His sufferings" (Phil. 3:10).

A mother is in pain when she is delivering a child, but the joy of having the child transforms pain into pleasure (see John 16:2–22). Whatever suffering we experience for the sake of Jesus not only should give us joy today but will give us future glory when we see our Lord. "Beloved, do not think it strange concerning the fiery trial which is to try you, as though some strange thing happened to you; but rejoice to the extent that you partake of Christ's sufferings, that when His glory is revealed, you may also be glad with exceeding joy" (1 Peter 4:12–13). Suffering and glory go together in the life of the dedicated Christian, and as the song tells us, "It will be worth it all when we see Jesus."

But something else is involved: when we suffer for the sake of Jesus, *it makes us more like Jesus!* Paul assures us that "tribulation produces perseverance; and perseverance, character; and character, hope. Now hope does not disappoint, because the love of God has been poured out in our hearts by the Holy Spirit who was given to us" (Rom. 5:3–5). Suffering works *for* us and not against us because the power of Christ rests upon us (2 Cor. 12:9). What a paradox! Our physical pain can produce spiritual maturity, and our weakness can produce strength! During our years of itinerant ministry, my wife and I have met some marvelous Christians in many parts of the world, and they have ministered richly to us. We were surprised to discover how many of them carried painful burdens and disappointments, but the triumph of their faith gave them joy and power in ministry. We have also met hidden heroes of faith in the churches we have served.

Consider how Paul dealt with this thorn in the flesh and let's follow his example:

- He looked upon his thorn in the flesh as a gift from God.
- He listened for God's message about the thorn.
- He accepted God's will concerning the purpose of the thorn.
- He depended on God's grace in handling the thorn.
- He experienced from the thorn strength out of weakness and joy out of pain.

More than anything else, Paul wanted the power of Christ to rest upon him (2 Cor. 12: 9). The word translated "rest upon" is related to the word "tent," and it pictures God's overshadowing "glory cloud" as in the Jewish tabernacle and on the Mount of Transfiguration (Matt. 17:5). The angel Gabriel used this image when speaking to Mary: "the power of the highest will overshadow you" (Luke 1:35). Her body would be the tabernacle for the miraculous conception of the Son of God. The believer's body is the temple of God (1 Cor. 6:19–20), and as we yield to Him, He uses us and glorifies His name. His cloud of glory hovers over us, guides and protects us, and we have nothing to fear.

Personal afflictions need not be a barrier to Christian service. If we are established in God's grace (Heb. 13:9) and have regular access to His throne of grace (Heb. 4:14–16), then we may serve the Lord as He directs us. Phillips Brooks said it best: "Do not pray for easy lives. Pray to be better men and women. Do not ask for tasks equal to your powers. Ask for powers equal to your tasks."

paradox

3

The More We Give,
the More We Receive

*I have coveted no one's silver or gold or apparel. Yes, you yourselves
know that these hands have provided for my necessities, and for
those who were with me. I have shown you in every way, by laboring like this, that you must support the weak. And remember the
words of the Lord Jesus, that He said, "It is more blessed to give
than to receive." (Acts 20:33–35)*

*Give, and it shall be given to you: good measure, pressed down,
shaken together, and running over will be put into your bosom,
for with the same measure that you use, it will be measured back
to you. (Luke 6:38)*

"BLESS" AND "BLESSING" are important words in the believer's
vocabulary, not only when we worship and pray, but also when
we give. But what *is* a blessing? Paul initially thought his thorn
in the flesh was a painful burden, but it turned out to be just the
blessing he needed (2 Cor. 12:7–10). Joseph was sure that his time
of confinement in Egypt was a mistake, but he discovered that it
fit right in with God's timetable when he became second ruler in
the land. The apostle Peter opposed our Lord's going to the cross,

but then he discovered that the cross was one of the greatest of all blessings God ever gave mankind.

Anything our Lord is, says, or does that edifies us and helps us to glorify Him is a blessing from God's hand. To know and share in God's character, God's word, and God's works is to be blessed, and to allow them to work in our lives and help others is to be blessed even more. As we walk with the Lord, we experience various stages of blessing; and to grow in the grace and knowledge of the Lord is to go from blessing to blessing. "And of His fullness we have all received, and grace for grace" (John 1:16). God prepares us for what He has prepared for us. But we are not reservoirs; we are channels — channels of blessing to bring the blessings of the Lord to others.

If you will read and ponder carefully the verses on page 21, you will find that there are at least three aspects of the blessing of the Lord: receiving God's blessing, sharing God's blessing, and glorifying God because of the blessing.

It Is a Great Blessing to Receive God's Gifts

Since the day of my birth, I have been surrounded by the multitude of the blessings the Lord has built into His marvelous creation. Each day I have sunlight to help me see and to help plants and people grow. I have air to breathe, food to eat, water to drink and to use for bathing, and a host of other useful gifts that enable me to enjoy life and get my work done. It's unfortunate that people made in God's image sometimes take these blessings for granted when we ought to be praising and thanking the Lord. "Then God saw everything that He had made, and indeed it was very good" (Gen. 1:31). "Oh, how great is Your goodness, which You have laid up for those who fear You, which You have prepared for those who trust in You in the presence of the sons of men!" (Ps. 31:19). This includes the remarkable body He designed for us. Read Psalm 139 and see what David thought of God's handiwork in the human body. God "gives us richly all things to enjoy" (1 Tim. 6:17), and yet people repeatedly ignore the goodness of the Lord God, abuse their bodies, lay waste the environment, and continue damaging and destroying His world.

"Every good gift and every perfect gift is from above, and comes down from the Father of lights, with whom there is no variation or shadow of turning" (James 1:17). What God gives is good and the way He gives it is good. He gives constantly and there is no change in His character. The gracious God of heaven prepared all these earthly blessings for us, and then He sent His Son Jesus to bless His people with "every spiritual blessing in the heavenly places in Christ" (Eph. 1:3). "He who did not spare His own Son, but delivered Him up for us all, how shall He not with Him also freely give us all things?" (Rom. 8:32). Each day we should frequently look up and thank the God who "gives to all life, breath, and all things" (Acts 17:25).

But we should also look back and give thanks for our ancestors without whom we could never have arrived in this world. When I was born, the doctor told my mother she would never raise me past the age of two — but the Lord had other plans. My Swedish great-grandfather (whom I never knew) prayed that there would be a preacher of the gospel in every generation of our family, *and there has been!* I was the candidate for my generation, so the Lord kept me alive.

Looking back, I thank God for my teachers in church, the public schools, and universities, and for the librarians who helped to develop my love for books and reading. This is not an autobiography, so I won't go into detail, but a host of people played important roles in preparing me for adulthood and ministry, and I thank God for them. It is indeed a blessing to receive! Most of all,

I thank Jesus Christ my Lord for giving Himself on the cross that I might be saved. An unsaved person might look at the pattern of my life and think it was a wrinkled and torn patchwork quilt, but quite the opposite is true. As my wife and I look back, we see the hand of God everywhere, and we give thanks. Yes, it is a great blessing to receive the gifts of God that make life and eternal life and abundant life possible, but there is something even better.

It Is a Greater Blessing to Share God's Gifts with Others

One day as He was teaching, Jesus said, "It is more blessed to give than to receive" (Acts 20:35), a statement that must have startled His listeners. What He said was never recorded by Matthew, Mark, Luke, or John; but when Paul first heard this statement quoted by some unnamed believer, he filed it away in his heart and quoted it one day to the Ephesian elders.

It doesn't surprise me that Paul latched on to this statement, for if there was ever a man who knew how to give, it was Paul. He later wrote to the Ephesians, "Let him that stole steal no longer, but rather let him labor, working with his hands what is good, that he may have something to give him who has need" (4:28). There are three ways to get money: stealing it (which includes counterfeiting), earning it, or receiving it as a gift. Paul encourages us to work, not just to pay our bills but *so that we may be able to give to others!* Paul knew what he was talking about because he labored with his own hands to help support himself and his fellow workers (Acts 20:34)

Starting with Exodus 20:17, the Scriptures warn us against covetousness, a commandment that is repeated in Deuteronomy 5:21. "He who is greedy for gain troubles his own house," says Proverbs 15:27; and Jesus warned His disciples, "Take heed and beware of covetousness, for one's life does not consist in the abundance of the things he possesses" (Luke 12:15). Hebrews 13:5 says, "Let your conduct be without covetousness, and be content with such things as you have. For He Himself has said, 'I will never leave you nor forsake you.'" The quotation is from Deuteronomy 31:6, 8, and Joshua 1:5.

Just as anger in the heart is murder (Matt. 25:21–26), and lust in the heart is adultery (Matt. 5:27–30), so greed in the heart is idolatry (Col. 3:5). Professed Christians who worship money, people, things, and themselves are as much idolaters as the people in the Bible who worshiped Baal. Psalm 115:1–8 warns us that, spiritually speaking, idolaters become like the gods they worship — unable to speak, hear, see, smell, or move. Matthew 13:22 warns us that "the deceitfulness of riches" will choke the seed of God's word sown in our hearts and make us fruitless. If we are covetous, we may become rich; but we may also fall into temptation, ruin, and destruction, for "the love of money is a root of all kinds of evil" (1 Tim. 6:9–10).

The Bible says much about helping the poor and protecting them from being exploited by ungodly rich and powerful people. Jesus pointed out that when we give to the poor, we are actually giving to Him! "Assuredly, I say to you, inasmuch as you did it to one of the least of these My brethren, you did it to Me" (Matt. 25:40).

One reason why giving results in receiving is that giving makes us more like God and opens our hearts to receive more blessing to give to others. The Lord knows He can trust with His wealth generous believers who give Him all the glory. "For you know the grace of our Lord Jesus Christ, that though He was rich, yet for your sakes He became poor, that you through His poverty might become rich" (2 Cor. 8:9). Grace and greed simply will not dwell in the same heart. The law of Moses commanded the people of Israel to give to the poor, and the believers in the New Testament churches followed their example and so should we (Acts 4:34–35; 11:27–30; Rom. 15:25–27; 2 Cor. 8–9).

Systematic sacrificial giving sets us free from bondage to this passing world, "the lust of the flesh, the lust of the eyes, and the pride of life" (1 John 2:15–17). It reminds us that every good thing we are, have, and do comes from God. Accumulating luxuries instead of majoring on necessities only multiplies our worries (Matt. 6:25–34). Abraham, Isaac, and Jacob were all rich men, and so were David and Joseph of Arimathea; but they possessed the wealth, the wealth did not possess them. A dedicated Christian may have wealth and yet be free from the "money maladies" that plague people — pride, arrogance, worry, and selfishness.

It's important that our giving not be advertised; that only inflates our pride even more. "Take heed that you do not do your charitable deeds before men, to be seen by them. Otherwise you have no reward from your Father in heaven. . . . But when you do a charitable deed, do not let your left hand know what your right hand is doing, that your charitable deed may be in secret, and your Father who sees in secret will Himself reward you openly" (Matt. 6:1, 3–4). We cannot receive our reward three times — once from God, once from our acquaintances, and once from ourselves. If my right hand knows what my left hand is doing, it will pat me on the back!

When we cheerfully give to the Lord (2 Cor. 9:7), we are actually making investments that pay rich dividends not only in this life but in our heavenly life to come in glory. That is our next topic.

It Will Be the Greatest Blessing When We See Jesus in Glory

Whatever we give to the Lord, He has first given to us. "But who am I, and who are my people, that we should be able to offer so willingly as this?" asked David. "For all things come from You, and of Your own we have given You" (1 Chron. 29:14). God gives to us and we in turn give back to Him as we give to others (Matt. 25:40). Jesus instructed us, "Do not lay up for yourselves treasures on earth, where moth and rust destroy and where thieves break in and steal; but lay up for yourselves treasures in heaven, where neither moth nor rust destroys and where thieves do not break in and steal. For where your treasure is, there your heart will be also" (Matt. 6:19–21). If you really want to know where your heart is, page through your check book and see how much has been invested in the bank of heaven.

It is more blessed to give than to receive because giving is an act of faith, and "without faith it is impossible to please Him" (Heb. 11:6). The Father said of Jesus, "This is My beloved Son in whom I am well pleased" (Matt. 3:17). I want Him to say that of me! We all want God to be "working in [us] that which is well-pleasing in His sight, through Jesus Christ, to whom be glory forever and ever" (Heb. 13:21). If we give only to receive and not to be a blessing to others to the glory of God, then our motives are not godly. The well-known Christian industrialist R. G. LeTourneau (1888–1969) used to say, "If you give because it pays, it won't pay." I have a copy of his autobiography *Mover of Men and Mountains,* and each time I look at the photographs of his huge inventions, from house-movers to missile launchers, I shake my head in disbelief. He gave God the glory and simply said, "I am just a mechanic whom the Lord has blessed." He autographed my copy and added "Matthew 6:33." What a verse — and what a man!

Yes, there are rewards on earth today for God's faithful people, but there will also be rewards in heaven. "For we shall all stand before the judgment seat of Christ" (Rom. 14:10). "For we must all appear before the judgment seat of Christ, that each one may receive the things done in the body, according to what he has done, whether good or bad" (2 Cor. 5:10). "Therefore judge nothing before the time, until the Lord comes, who will both bring to light the hidden things of darkness and reveal the counsels of the heart; and then each one's praise will come from God" (1 Cor. 4:5). Faithful servants of God will receive "the crown of glory that does not fade away" (1 Peter 5:4).

The key to a joyful life now and a blessed future in heaven is *faithfulness.* "Moreover it is required in stewards that one be found faithful" (1 Cor. 4:2). Many people who are considered successful on earth today may be classified as *unfaithful* when they arrive in heaven and meet their Lord. Paul's counsel to Timothy needs to be heeded today: "Preach the word! Be ready in season and out of season. Convince, rebuke, exhort, with all longsuffering and teaching. . . . But you be watchful in all things, endure afflictions, do the work of an evangelist, fulfill your ministry" (2 Tim. 4:2, 5). We are living in a world that rejects God's Son and God's truth and opposes God's people, and we must be faithful. The more we give now of ourselves, our time, and our possessions, the more we will receive now and for all eternity.

The words of Jesus to His church in Smyrna are applicable to us today: "I know your works, tribulation, and poverty (but you are rich)" (Rev. 2:9). What a precious parenthesis!

When We Choose to Go Down, God Lifts Us Up

Pride goes before destruction, and a haughty spirit before a fall. (Prov. 16:18)

He has shown you, O man, what is good; and what does the LORD require of you but to do justly, to love mercy, and to walk humbly with your God? (Micah 6:8)

But he who is greatest among you shall be your servant. And whoever exalts himself will be humbled, and he who humbles himself will be exalted. (Matt. 23:11–12)

Now there was also a dispute among them, as to which of [the disciples] should be considered greatest. And [Jesus] said to them, "The kings of the Gentiles exercise lordship over them, and those who exercise authority over them are called 'benefactors.' But not so among you; on the contrary, he who is greatest among you, let him be as the younger, and he who governs as he who serves. . . . I am among you as the One who serves." (Luke 22:24–27)

For I say, through the grace given to me, to everyone who is among you, not to think of himself more highly than he ought to think, but to think soberly, as God has dealt to each one a measure of faith. (Rom. 12:3)

> Let nothing be done through selfish ambition or conceit, but
> in lowliness of mind let each esteem others better than himself.
> (*Phil.* 2:3)

> Humble yourselves in the sight of the Lord, and He will lift you
> up. (*James* 4:10)

> Therefore humble yourselves under the mighty hand of God, that
> He may exalt you in due time. (1 *Peter* 5:6)

THE TWO LITTLE WORDS "UP" AND "DOWN" are important to
everybody. In their fascinating book *Metaphors We Live By*, George
Lakoff and Mark Johnson point out how these two "location
words" help us communicate truth. If you are healthy, you "feel
up to it," but if you are sickly, you feel "down" or "low." We speak of
"the peak of health" or a patient "sinking fast." People "come down"
with the flu or some other ailment. People are "depressed" (down)
or "on top of it" (up). A person "sinks" into a coma or "drops" dead.
When things are going well, we are "on top of the situation" and
"everything is up"; but when things are "going downhill," our spirits
"sink." We are supposed to "climb the ladder of success" and "keep
looking up." I think you get the point.[1]

For the most part, today's culture wants nothing to do with
humility but joyfully promotes pride. People respected Mother
Teresa but were more excited over rock stars and movie stars. In
our newspapers we have detailed obituaries extolling the greatness
of the dead; and advertisers in the other sections of the newspaper
keep reminding us that we too can be important and successful if
only we use their products. "Pride is the ground in which all the
other sins grow and the parent from which all the other sins come,"

---

1   George Lakoff and Mark Johnson, *Metaphors We Live By* (Chicago:
University of Chicago Press, 1980), 14–18.

wrote Bible scholar William Barclay. King Saul's pride turned him into an envious tyrant and motivated him to hate David and try to kill him. David's pride moved him to take a census of Israel, and as a result 70,000 people died (2 Sam. 24:15), and the pride of David's son Absalom led to his death and David's deep sorrow (2 Sam. 13–19).

If Christians want to "go up," they first must "go down" and obey James 4:10: "Humble yourselves in the sight of the Lord, and He will lift you up." James gives us three instructions to obey if we want God to lift us up in victory for His glory.

We Must Cultivate True Humility

The word "humility" comes from a Latin word that means "low, near the ground." Proud people elevate themselves and thrive on compliments and special attention, but the Lord hates pride (Prov. 6:16–17; 8:13).

According to the biblical record, pride was the first sin committed when the angel Lucifer rebelled against God and became Satan (Isa. 14:12–15). The first sin on earth was committed by Eve because she believed Satan's promise that, if she ate of the tree, she would be like God (Gen. 3:1–8).

A feeling of pride is often the first step toward committing sin. People who constantly think only of promoting and pleasing themselves become their own god and sin against the Lord, themselves, and other people. The pride of King Saul robbed him of the blessing of God, and the pride of David's son Absalom turned him into a rebel and led to his untimely death (2 Sam. 15–18). Because of his pride, King Herod Agrippa I was eaten by worms and died (Acts 12:20–23). "God resists the proud but gives grace to the humble" (Prov. 3:34; James 4:6; 1 Peter 5:5).

There is a false humility that is disgusting and certainly grieves the Lord. It occurs when people debase themselves because they want others to praise them. I have heard people say, "Please don't ask me to sing, I just don't have that ability." But everybody knew they did have ability, given to them by the Lord. But they used this approach because they wanted to be begged and pampered. Beg them to serve and you might discourage the truly dedicated volunteers, but if you ignore them and enlist somebody else, the braggart will sulk and cause trouble.

It has well been said that humility does not mean thinking poorly of ourselves *but just not thinking of ourselves at all!* Isaiah knew his own faults, but when God called him, he said, "Here am I! Send me" (Isa. 6:8). The Lord cleansed him and equipped him to do His work. Growing in humility is a matter between the believer and God, who alone knows the human heart and forgives us, teaches us, and molds us. He gave the apostle Paul a thorn in the flesh to keep him from getting proud (2 Cor. 12:1–10). Humility is that quality of character that, when we know we have it, we have lost it. And believers who are proud of being humble are dangerous to have around. When pride imitates humility, the devil is at work.

Of course, the greatest example of humility is our Lord Jesus Christ (Phil. 2:5–12), and the more we learn of Him and love Him, the more we will become like Him. Consider what He said about Himself.

- "The Son can do nothing of Himself." (John 5:19)
- "I do not seek My own will." (John 5:30)
- "For I have come down from heaven, not to do My own will." (John 6:38)
- "My doctrine is not Mine, but His who sent Me." (John 7:16)

- "I do nothing of Myself; but as My Father taught Me, I speak these things." (John 8:28)
- "I proceeded forth and came from God." (John 8:42)
- "I do not seek My own glory." (John 8:50)
- "The words that I speak to you I do not speak on My own authority." (John 14:10)

We mature spiritually as we spend time daily meditating on the word of God, praying, giving, and serving others. As a result we come to know the Lord better and also ourselves. Humble people know themselves, accept themselves, and give themselves to serve God and glorify Him. It is essential that we confess our sins, but we do not become humble by looking at ourselves. "The heart is deceitful above all things, and desperately wicked; who can know it?" (Jer. 17:9). We cannot always trust our own self-examinations. We need to follow the example of David when he prayed, "Search me, O God, and know my heart; try me, and know my anxieties; and see if there is any wicked way in me, and lead me in the way everlasting" (Ps. 139:23–24). He prayed in Psalm 19:12, "Cleanse me from secret faults," meaning "the sins I did not even know I committed."

We must have a healthy examination of the heart, led by the Spirit using the Scriptures, but we must avoid what Dr. Martyn Lloyd-Jones called "morbid introspection."[2] If we are not careful, we can spend so much time focusing on our sins that we give Satan opportunity to accuse us and discourage us. Sins that we have confessed and forsaken our Father has forgiven and forgotten (1 John 1:9; Heb. 8:12; 10:17). And so should we! Meditate on Zechariah 3:1–5.

---

2   D. Martyn Lloyd-Jones, *Faith on Trial* (Grand Rapids: Eerdmans 1965), 66.

Do I have true humility? I can find out by answering these questions honestly. How do I respond to compliments and criticisms? If I am being completely ignored, do I deliberately call attention to myself? Do I frequently compare myself to others and inwardly criticize them and praise myself? Pride makes us envious and envy makes us critical. Do I judge others more severely than I judge myself? Do I major in criticism or seek ways to compliment and encourage others? Do I forgive others or carry grudges? Do I rejoice when I have opportunities to help others anonymously, or do I have to blow a trumpet and call attention to myself (Matt. 6:1–4)? If God has given me enviable intelligence, do I call attention to it, or simply use it to help others? Anglican clergyman Jeremy Taylor (1613–1667) wrote, "To be proud of learning is the greatest ignorance in the world." "Pride makes us artificial," wrote Thomas Merton (1915–1968), "and humility makes us real."

Consider these statements from Scripture:

- "Though the Lord is on high, yet He regards the lowly; but the proud He knows from afar." (Ps. 138:6)
- "For thus says the High and Lofty One who inhabits eternity, whose name is holy: 'I dwell in the high and lofty place, with him who has a contrite and humble spirit, to revive the spirit of the humble, and to revive the heart of the contrite ones.'" (Isa. 57:15)
- "But on this one will I look: on him who is poor and of a contrite spirit, and who trembles at My word." (Isa. 66:2b).
- "Blessed are the poor in spirit for theirs is the kingdom of heaven." (Matt. 5:3) (Notice Jesus did not say "the poor spirited" with their artificial humility, but "the poor in spirit," the truly humble who know how great God is and how bankrupt they are!)

We Must Practice Complete Honesty

To humble ourselves "in the sight of the Lord" simply means to live honestly before the Lord and before others. The opposite is hypocrisy, assuming various roles and pretending from time to time to be something we are not. "He who covers his sins will not prosper," Solomon warned (Prov. 28:13). David covered his sins for nearly a year, and suffered greatly (Ps. 32:3–5). Achan robbed the Lord and buried the loot under his tent, and he and his family (who must have conspired with him) were found out and lost their lives (Josh. 7). Ananias and Sapphira also died because they robbed God and lied about it (Acts 5:1–11). Dishonesty is dangerous.

God keeps His eyes on His people. "The eyes of the LORD are in every place, keeping watch on the evil and the good" (Prov. 15:3). The Jews ridiculed the pagan idols for having eyes and not being able to see (Ps. 115:5), but there were times when Israel sinned deliberately and openly, knowing full well that the Lord saw all they did and would discipline them. Have we ever done that? "He who planted the ear, shall He not hear? He who formed the eye, shall He not see?" (Ps. 94:9).

We can live with humility "in the sight of the Lord" because He watches us *for our own protection.* "Behold the eye of the LORD is on those who fear Him, on those who hope in His mercy" (Ps. 33:18). From crossing the Red Sea and leaving Egypt to crossing the Jordan River into Canaan, the people of Israel had God's protection and provision day after day for forty years, and then He helped them defeat their enemies and claim their Promised Land. My wife and I have traveled thousands of miles in ministry and God has graciously brought us home safely at the end of each meeting. Whether we were on the highway or in the air, we were always confident of His care. Sometimes there were delays and even cancellations, but our lives, our luggage, and our times were all in His capable hand (Ps. 31:15). The Lord watched over the land of Israel (Deut. 11) and kept it safe and fruitful as long as the people were obeying His law.

The Lord also keeps His eyes on us *for our direction in life.* "I will instruct you and teach you in the way you should go; I will guide you with My eye" (Ps. 32:8). God does not want us to be like horses that are prone to rush ahead or mules that are stubbornly prone to lag behind (Ps. 32:9). Better we are like sheep who know their shepherd's voice and obediently follow Him (John 10:4).

The all-seeing eyes of the Lord also assure us of *inspection.* "For His eyes are on the ways of man, and He sees all his steps" (Job 34:21; see Ps. 139:1–6, 23–24). When I was a lad, I could not walk out the front door and head for grade school without first being carefully scrutinized by my mother. Were my hands and face clean? Did I brush my teeth? Did I have a clean handkerchief? God wants His children to be at their best so they may do their best. That is one of the purposes of a daily devotional time with the Lord, so that He might inspect us and help us see ourselves as we really are (James 1:21–25).

So far I have been negative, but let me assure you that the watching eyes of the Lord also speak of *affection.* Loving parents keep their eyes on their children because they love them and rejoice to see how they are developing in their skills. When our two daughters were young and taking piano lessons, my wife and I attended the annual recital and proudly listened to them play. What a high hour it was in heaven and on earth when Jesus was baptized and His Father said, "This is My beloved Son, in whom I am well pleased" (Matt. 3:17). I trust that from time to time the Father can look down at me and my ministry and say the same thing!

The Father also keeps His eyes on us for *correction,* just as a coach watches the team playing or parents their children eating dinner. Nehemiah prayed that the Lord would keep His eyes on the people of Israel and correct them, for they had sinned (Neh. 1). He and his people were going to Jerusalem to rebuild the walls, and they needed His loving care. God does not watch us the way a policeman watches a prisoner but the way a loving parent watches a child. He wants us to learn how to glorify Him in what we say and do.

God's goal for His people is *perfection*. "Therefore you shall be perfect, just as your Father in heaven is perfect" (Matt. 5:48). Jesus was not talking about sinless perfection, because we will not reach that goal until we see Jesus (1 John 3:1–3). Our Lord is talking about Christian maturity and completeness of life. The Greek word is *katartizō* and it has several meanings; among them are these four: to equip soldiers for battle, to rig a ship for sailing, to set a broken bone, and to repair a fishing net. The Holy Spirit uses several "spiritual tools" to help God's children mature, among them the inspired word of God (2 Tim. 3:16–17), prayer (2 Cor. 13:9; 1 Thess. 3:10), the ministry of the church (Eph. 4:11–16), and personal suffering (1 Peter 5:10). The prayer of Hebrews 13:20–21 is greatly needed today: "Now may the God of peace . . . make you complete in every good work to do His will, working in you what is well pleasing in His sight, through Jesus Christ, to whom be glory forever and ever."

We Must Expect Joyful Victory

By faith, we go down in humility and God raises us up in victory. But He does not lift us up so that we may be praised but so that we may serve others and glorify Jesus. "But he who is greatest among you shall be your servant," said Jesus (Matt. 23:11), and He demonstrated it by going down low enough to wash His disciples' feet (John 13). Andrew Murray wrote that "there is nothing so divine as being the servant and helper of all." Humility leads to obedience, and obedience manifests love. The apostle Paul called this "serving the Lord with all humility" (Acts 20:19). Our service may not be immediately appreciated or rewarded on earth, but it is recorded in heaven where one day we will receive our reward.

When I recall the Christians who truly were a blessing to me and others, I note that each of them had a humble mind and a servant's heart. When I was a young pastor, I often phoned or visited older pastors in our area to get some counsel. They must have considered me a pest, but they listened patiently and shared their wisdom. Years later, the young pastors were phoning *me!* What a joy it has been to listen to them, encourage them, and pray with them. "Poverty of spirit empties a man," said Charles Spurgeon, "and so makes him ready to be filled."

Abraham and Sarah were old and unknown, yet God chose them to be the founders of the Hebrew nation. They humbled themselves and God lifted them up. Joseph humbled himself to be a servant in the Egyptian prison and God elevated him to be the second ruler of the land. Moses was a fugitive from Egypt and a humble shepherd in Midian, yet God called him to deliver the Jews from bondage and give them His law. Joshua was Moses' humble servant, yet he became head of the army and Moses' successor. David was a humble shepherd, but the Lord used him to defeat a giant and lead an army. Review Hebrews 11 and see how many people humbled themselves and were promoted to do great things for God and His people. But remember that God lifted them up, not to be famous, but that they might minister to others and glorify Him. They were servants and not celebrities.

Mary, the mother of Jesus, understood this truth, for she sang, "He has put down the mighty from their thrones, and exalted the lowly. He has filled the hungry with good things, and the rich He has sent away empty" (Luke 1:52–53).

"It is not humility to underrate yourself," said Charles Spurgeon. "Humility is to think of yourself as God thinks of you. It is to feel that, if we have talents, God has given them to us. And let it be seen that, like freight in a vessel, they tend to sink us low. The more we have, the lower we ought to lie."[3]

---

3   C. H. Spurgeon, *The New Park Street Pulpit*, vol. 2 (Grand Rapids: Baker, 1990), 350.

5

Our Foolishness Leads Us to God's Wisdom

Humble yourselves in the sight of the Lord, and He will lift you up. (James 4:10)

For the message of the cross is foolishness to those who are perishing, but to us who are being saved it is the power of God. For it is written, "I will destroy the wisdom of the wise, and bring to nothing the understanding of the prudent." Where is the wise? Where is the scribe? Where is the disputer of this age? Has not God made foolish the wisdom of this world? For since in the wisdom of God, the world through wisdom did not know God, it pleased God through the foolishness of the message preached to save those who believe. For Jews request a sign, and Greeks seek after wisdom; but we preach Christ crucified, to the Jews a stumbling block and to the Greeks foolishness, but to those who are called, both Jews and Greeks, Christ the power of God and the wisdom of God. Because the foolishness of God is wiser than men, and the weakness of God is stronger than men. For you see your calling, brethren, that not many wise according to the flesh, not many mighty, not many noble are called. But God has chosen the foolish things of the world to put to shame the wise, and God has chosen the weak things of the world to put to shame the

*mighty; and the base things of the world and the things which
are despised God has chosen, and the things which are not, to
bring to nothing the things that are, that no flesh should glory in
His presence. But of Him you are in Christ Jesus, who became for
us wisdom from God and righteousness and sanctification and
redemption — that as it is written, He who glories, let him glory
in the LORD. (1 Cor. 1:18–31)*

ACCORDING TO THE JOURNALISTS, we are now living in the
Information Age. We can push a few buttons and get information
about almost any person, place, thing, or event. We are glutted
with facts and theories, but starved for wisdom. And so-called
brilliant people continue to say and do dumb things and get paid
for it. The Christian poet William Cowper wrote that "knowledge
is proud that he has learned so much, while wisdom is humble that
he knows no more." Eric Hoffer wrote in *The Passionate State of
Mind*, "The hardest thing to cope with is not selfishness or vanity
or deceitfulness, but sheer stupidity." I sometimes recall the words
of poet T. S. Eliot from his *Choruses from The Rock*:

> Where is the wisdom we have lost in knowledge?
> Where is the knowledge we have lost in information?

There were serious problems in the church at Corinth because
some of the members were boasting of their knowledge but un-
aware of their ignorance. They were trying to mix the wisdom of
this world with the wisdom of God and the formula was definitely
wrong. They were proud of what they thought they knew, but
paupers when it came to knowing God's wisdom.

I have been privileged to pastor three churches, minister with
three different parachurch organizations, and serve on several
boards. And I have learned that the people of God today often

make the same mistakes the Corinthians made. Instead of opening our Bibles, calling a prayer meeting, and seeking God's wisdom, we hurriedly "share ideas" and ask how the world is getting things done. Lacking the leading of the Spirit, and ignorant of the difference between wisdom and knowledge, the committee soon disagrees and ends up with carnal division instead of godly decision.

Sixteen times in I Corinthians 1–2, Paul uses the word "wisdom," and five times he uses the word "foolishness." These are the two key words of our meditation.

To the World, God's Wisdom Is Foolishness

Alfred North Whitehead (1861–1947) was a brilliant philosopher and mathematician, and yet he rejected the Christian message. He said that he had given up on the Bible and that there was "no longer much of anything in it for him." He preferred reading Plato.[1] "I consider Christian theology to be one of the great disasters of the human race," he said.[2] Frankly, I have read Whitehead and have learned from him, but his rejection of the Christian faith has always grieved me, especially when he says, "As for the Christian theology, can you imagine anything more appallingly idiotic than the Christian idea of heaven?"[3]

Saul of Tarsus was also a brilliant man who stumbled over Christ and the cross. But one day he was blinded that he might see and he trusted Jesus as his Savior and Lord and became Paul the apostle (Acts 9). "For the message of the cross is foolishness to those who are perishing, but to us who are being saved it is the

---

1   Lucian Price, *The Dialogues of Alfred North Whitehead* (New York: Little, Brown, and Co., 1954), 182–83.

2   Ibid., 174.

3   Ibid., 277.

power of God" (1 Cor. 1:18). Paul suffered persecution because he preached Christ and the cross, and he boasted in the cross as the power of God for the salvation of lost sinners (Gal. 6:12–14).

Paul's living identification with the crucified Christ was the secret of His life and service. He wrote, "I have been crucified with Christ; it is no longer I who live, but Christ lives in me" (Gal. 2:20). Because of Christ, Paul was a transformed man. The Bible does not encourage ignorance; it encourages us to grow in wisdom so that we will know how to make the right use of knowledge. Science has a right to boast of its many achievements, and I for one give thanks for the good things science has contributed to our lives, especially in the field of medicine. But it is wrong for science to leave out the Lord and take credit for what He has given us. The Lord wants us to enjoy His blessings, but we should give Him the glory. We may buy sleep *but not peace of heart*. We can remove stains and wash off dirt, but apart from the Lord's power, *we cannot renew the mind or cleanse the human heart*.

As I write these words, the newscasters are telling us that there are forty-four critical "danger spots" in our world where innocent people are being killed, valuable property is being destroyed, and freedom is being taken away. There is no man-made medicine available to change the sinful human heart, but "the blood of Jesus Christ His Son cleanses us from all sin" (1 John 1:7).

There are many accounts in the Bible of the foolishness of mankind in rejecting the wisdom of God and depending on the "wisdom" of this world. Of course, it all begins with Eve disobeying the Lord and influencing her husband Adam to join her in eating the fruit of the forbidden tree (Gen. 3; 1 Tim. 2:14). Next came the foolish builders of the tower of Babel, who defied God and built a tower (Gen. 11:1–9). The whole enterprise failed because the people rebelled against God. From the confusion of Babel in Genesis to the destruction of Babylon in Revelation 18–19, every enterprise of man failed that was not planned and directed by the Lord. "There is a way which seems right to a man, but its end is the way of death" (Prov. 14:12).

Jesus gave a parable about a successful farmer who ended up a fool because he forgot that one day he would die (Luke 12:13–21). Our Lord also told about a man who built his house on the sand and lost everything, when he could have built on rock and saved everything (Matt. 7:24–27). To build on rock means to obey the will of God. It is foolish not to have Jesus Christ as the foundation of life. Jesus called the five bridesmaids foolish because they failed to bring oil for their lamps as they waited for the bridegroom to arrive (Matt. 25:1–13). Acts 27 describes the destruction of a ship in a storm because the leaders were foolish and refused to obey God's will. Paul warned the centurion, the owner of the ship, and the helmsman that if they set sail, the ship would be wrecked in a storm. But the centurion believed the "experts" rather than Paul and the majority of the passengers voted to set sail. When a south wind began to blow softly (Acts 27:13), the leaders were sure it was safe to sail, but they sailed right into the storm! Of course, we must remember the biggest fool of all: "The fool has said in his heart, 'There is no God'" (Ps. 14:1).

There is a vast difference between the *knowledge* of this world and the *wisdom* of this world. Nowhere does the Bible condemn human knowledge, for the Lord created a marvelous universe, a superb planet earth, and an astonishing man and woman. He built into His creation laws and principles that are so accurate we can build our entire scientific endeavors upon them. We were created after the image of God and given brains to think with so we could exercise dominion over creation, enjoying and employing the treasures and pleasures of His handiwork (Gen. 1:26–30; Ps. 8). Wisdom is the right use of knowledge, making the most of God's gifts as He commanded us, all for His glory. It is unfortunate that our world is being unwisely used and abused so that human bodies and divinely supplied resources are being defiled and destroyed. Air and water are polluted; plants and animals are wastefully destroyed as are valuable minerals; and the environment God has given us is being wasted.

People who live only by the wisdom of this world think that Christians are fools for believing the Bible and living by faith, but the "scientific world" has experimented and written their own "bibles." Have they forgotten that the same God who wrote the Bible also wrote into the universe (including planet earth) the scientific principles that keep the machinery running? The laws of science are the laws of God, and if NASA had ignored those laws, there would have been no successful ventures into space. Whether it be for saving a marriage, raising children, holding a job, running a business, or building a church, God's wisdom points the way to real success: "Unless the Lord builds the house, they labor in vain who build it" (Ps. 127:1).

To God, the World's Wisdom Is Foolishness

Paul states it boldly: "Although they knew God, they did not glorify Him as God, nor were thankful, but became futile in their thoughts and their foolish hearts were darkened. Professing to be wise, they became fools" (Rom. 1:21–22). In their "wisdom," people replaced the living God with dead idols that they had manufactured themselves! The sociologists tell us that "religion" began with the worship of many gods and idols and worked its way up to faith in one true a living God, but just the opposite is true. Mankind began with a clear knowledge of the true God and rejected Him for the worship of gods they made themselves.

Our world today is filled with dead idols that control the lives of people, things such as money, property, movie stars, athletic teams, or heroes, status, authority, fame, achievement, pleasure, and pride of education, to name but a few. Some people have even made idols out of a religion, worshiping a "system" instead of the eternal God. Anything we trust and live for other than the true and living God is an idol and must be put out of our lives. Idolatry thrives on ignorant unbelief, while the worship of the true and living God thrives on faith and obedience.

Many of the world's "great" people feel that pride is the indispensable ingredient for achieving success. You must be somebody important and let others know how important you are. But Jesus says, "Blessed are the poor in spirit, for theirs is the kingdom of heaven" (Matt. 5:3); and King Solomon wrote, "When pride comes, then comes shame; but with the humble is wisdom" (Prov. 11:2). The truly great people in the Bible did not promote themselves but left it to the Lord. God told Joshua, "This day I will begin to exalt you in the sight of Israel" (Josh. 3:7). It was not easy to be successor to Moses, but Joshua left it in the hands of the Lord and succeeded to His glory.

Too often Christian leaders imitate the world and focus on promoting themselves instead of magnifying the Lord. "No sin cuts us off so effectively from God and our fellow man as the sin of pride," said Emil Brunner in a sermon. "That is the root of all sins — the magnifying of the ego."[4] It is unfortunate that some of the methods of the lost world are being brought into Christian ministries, while the wisdom of the Lord is being ignored.

Pity the Christian workers who never ask God to give wisdom but only that He would bless the clever plans they have made. David imitated the Philistines and had the ark of the Lord carried to Jerusalem on a cart rather than on the shoulders of the priests,

---

4   Emil Brunner, *The Great Invitation* (Philadelphia: Westminster Press, 1955), 61.

and the venture was a failure (2 Sam. 6). When King Rehoboam followed the counsel of his worldly minded young friends instead of that of the experienced elders, he divided the kingdom (1 Kings 12). More than one ministry has almost been destroyed by proud leaders who got their guidance from the world and not from the Lord. From my first day in seminary until this very day, I have sought the mind of the Lord; and though I have made my share of mistakes, He has graciously guided and provided and, I trust, been glorified.

We need as much of this world's knowledge as we can get, but we need the wisdom of the Lord to help us process it and use it. "Beware of the atmosphere of the classics," Robert Murray M'Cheyne wrote to a friend. "True, we ought to know them; but only as chemists handle poisons – to discover their qualities, not to infect their blood with them."[5] When I was a teenager and a new believer, one of the founders of Youth for Christ, Dr. Torrey Johnson, said to me, "Learn all you can, put it under the blood, and use it to the glory of the Lord." I followed his counsel and can guarantee that it works. Daniel and his three friends mastered the "wisdom" of the Babylonians but succeeded in maintaining a godly witness in a pagan land because they trusted the Lord for the wisdom they needed day by day.

To Christian Believers, God's Foolishness Is True Wisdom

People who are still lost in their sins consider the message of the gospel foolishness and the people who believe that message fools. Most of these people have never read the Bible or given serious thought to who Jesus is and what He can do for them. They build

---

5   Andrew A. Bonar, *Robert Murray M'Cheyne: Memoirs and Remains* (London: Banner of Truth Trust, 1966), 29.

their case on the agnostic flotsam and jetsam that they pick up here and there, and if invited to discuss the gospel, they excuse themselves because they have "more important things to do." To them, Jesus is only an unemployed Jewish carpenter who thought He was God and died as a criminal on a Roman cross. His followers convinced people that He had risen from the dead and returned to heaven, and many ignorant people believed them. To them, it is all foolishness from beginning to end.

We who are Christians must live as "wise fools." We are wise because we trust Jesus Christ and accept the word of God, even though the message of the cross seems like foolishness to unbelievers. To them we are fools. The gospel is a message of grace, and grace is something unsaved people cannot grasp. Why would God become man and suffer and die? How can another person's death affect people today? The cross looks like defeat, not victory! People are accustomed to do things for themselves and to work for what they want, and they stumble over the free gift of forgiveness. They wrestle with the facts of a shameful cross and a free gift of salvation but yet the logic of salvation eludes them. Only our prayers and the work of the Holy Spirit can enlighten them and bring fruit from the seeds we have planted. Salvation by grace may not seem logical from a human point of view, but this salvation is available — and it works! We don't push people into the kingdom *head* first; we pray them into the kingdom *heart* first.

Our dependence must be on the Holy Spirit (Acts 1:8). Paul mentions Him eight times in the first three chapters of 1 Corinthians, and what he wrote parallels what Jesus said to His disciples in the upper room (John 14:15–18; 15:26–16:15). The Spirit works in and through believers and convicts the unsaved of their guilt and need of Christ. We must not depend on clever approaches in presenting the gospel but only on the ministry of the Spirit (1 Cor. 2). We must be taught by the Spirit and led by the Spirit. Paul emphasizes the unadorned preaching of the gospel that clearly presents Jesus and the cross (1 Cor. 1:18–2:5). Why? So that Jesus Christ is glorified and not the preacher! The world's wisdom mixed with the gospel robs the message of its power (1 Cor. 1:18–23).

Some of the newspapers in Chicago called evangelist Dwight L. Moody "Crazy Moody" as he worked to win souls, but those writers and their newspapers are forgotten today and D. L. Moody's ministry goes on. Moody gave up a successful shoe business to devote himself to preaching the gospel, and God honored his faith and obedience. Pharaoh and the Egyptian army must have laughed as the Israelites came to the Red Sea, but God opened the sea and the Jews crossed on dry ground. The Egyptian army was drowned. The inhabitants of Jericho must have laughed at the Israelites as they marched around their city day after day, but it was Joshua and his people who had the last laugh when Jericho's walls collapsed and the city was captured (Josh. 6).

How important it is for God's people to be "wise fools" who are willing to be called "fools for Christ's sake" (1 Cor. 4:10) so that He will receive all the glory.

6

By Standing Still,
We Go Forward

Even the youths shall faint and be weary and the young men shall utterly fall, but those who wait on the LORD shall renew their strength; they shall mount up with wings as eagles, they shall run and not be weary, they shall walk and not faint. (Isa. 40:30–31)

And He said, "My Presence will go with you, and I will give you rest." (Exod. 33:14)

And I said, "Oh, that I had wings like a dove! For then I would fly away and be at rest." (Ps. 55:6)

Therefore I say to you, do not worry about your life, what you will eat or what you will drink; nor about your body, what you will put on. Is not life more than food and the body more than clothing? . . . Which of you by worrying can add one cubit to his stature? . . . But seek first the kingdom of God and His righteousness, and all these things shall be added to you. (Matt. 6:25, 27, 33)

Wait on the LORD; be of good courage, and He shall strengthen your heart; wait, I say, on the LORD. (Ps. 27:14)

My soul, wait silently for God alone, for my expectation is from Him. He only is my rock and my salvation; He is my defense: I shall not be moved. (Ps. 62:5–6)

The work of righteousness will be peace, and the effect of righteousness, quietness and assurance forever. (Isa. 32:17)

A UNIVERSITY PROFESSOR was meeting a famous Chinese lecturer in a crowded train station. After welcoming him, the professor said, "If we run to our gate, we can get the next train and save three minutes." The guest quietly asked, "And what significant thing shall we do with the three minutes that we are saving?" The professor's reply is not recorded, but it may have marked a turning point in his own education.

Here's a story from my own life. As guest preacher at a church, I spoke about slowing down and taking time to fellowship with the Lord each day. When I had finished the message, the worship leader stepped forward and announced, "We will now sing hymn number 325, 'Take Time to Be Holy,' verses 1 and 4." We did not even take time to sing all four verses, and we did nothing significant with the few minutes that we "saved." I was disappointed, because each of the verses related to a key point in my message.

I have traveled enough on land and in the air to know that people almost everywhere are in a hurry and want everything and everybody to get out of their way. The word "fast" is very important in our American vocabulary. Some highways provide "fast lanes" for cars carrying two or more people. Basketball has its "fast break" and baseball its "fastball," and we must not neglect "fast food" or making a "fast buck." I have spoken in churches where the service was scripted *to the second* so there would be time enough for the musicians to perform and the pastor to preach the announcements. There is rarely time left for the guest speaker to give the whole message he had prepared, though he was promised "plenty of time."

Yes, there are times in the Christian life when we must hurry; but the success of our occasional running depends on the success of our consistent daily resting, exercising, and eating. "Could you not watch one hour?" Jesus asked sleeping Peter in the Garden of Gethsemane (Mark 14:37).

There are at least four important lessons we must learn if we are to move forward effectively day by day, serving our Lord Jesus Christ but not running a ridiculous race.

We Must Learn to Be Still

"Be still, and know that I am God" (Ps. 46:10). The Father wants us to cultivate a quiet heart, but why? *Because the heart of every problem is the problem in the heart.* King Solomon wrote, "Keep your heart with all diligence, for out of it spring the issues of life" (Prov. 4:23); and Jesus warned, "No servant can serve two masters" (Luke 16:13). A divided heart is a disobedient heart and therefore a disturbed heart that enjoys no peace. "In returning and rest you shall be saved; in quietness and confidence shall be your strength" (Isa. 30: 15). If we are sincerely following Jesus, He will see to it that we enjoy the still waters (Ps. 23:2). Psalm 46:1–3 describes the dangerous waters that produce fear, but in verses 4–5 we have the river of God that brings rest.

In Matthew 11:28–30, Jesus invites weary and worried people to come to Him for rest. When we trust Him for salvation, He gives us rest, what Paul calls "peace with God" (Rom. 5:1). When we yield our all to Him day by day, we grow in our knowledge of Him and find a deeper rest, the "peace of God, which surpasses all understanding" (Phil. 4:7). Being human, we will experience difficult days when nothing seems to work out as it should. We may not feel like serving as we should, but the peace within us will encourage and strengthen us to get the job done. Living by our feelings is a treacherous thing and destroys living by faith. If the heart is disturbed, the will may be paralyzed and we may find it difficult to "serve the LORD with gladness" (Ps. 100:2). Take down the hymnal and sing your way through the old hymn "Be Still, My Soul." This is excellent medicine for a heart that is disappointed and discouraged.

We Must Learn to Sit Still

The French philosopher Blaise Pascal (1623–1662) wrote, "All the troubles of men are caused by one single thing, which is their inability to stay quietly in a room." After the widow Ruth had presented herself to Boaz, her kinsman redeemer, she received this valuable piece of advice from her mother-in-law Naomi: "Sit still, my daughter, until you know how the matter will turn out; for the man will not rest until he has concluded the matter this day" (Ruth 3:18). Boaz is a type of Jesus, our kinsman redeemer, and as the Lord works out His will for us, we must sit still, wait, and trust. Ruth and Naomi had never read Romans 8:28, but they certainly believed and practiced it! God works everything out for our good and His glory if only we will quit giving orders and get out of God's way. Psalm 46:10 can be translated, "Take your hands off." If we meddle with the will of God, we are in danger of missing what He has planned for us. God always gives His best to those who leave the choice with Him.

One of the frequently repeated questions in Scripture is, "How long?" David prayed in Psalm 13:1–2, "How long, O LORD? Will You forget me forever? How long will You hide Your face from me? How long shall I take counsel in my soul, having sorrow in my heart daily? How long will my enemy be exalted over me?" It is evident from Scripture that God is always at work for His people, but He is usually not in a hurry. Abraham and Sarah waited twenty-five years for their promised son to be born, and when they tried to hasten things, they got themselves and the nation of Israel into trouble. Moses was eighty years old before the Lord told him to return to Egypt and deliver his people. Our Lord Jesus Christ waited thirty years before launching into His public ministry. There is a time to work and there is a time to wait, and we must know the difference.

I had a friend in seminary who, like me, was both a student and a pastor, which meant having a challenging schedule. Some of the people in his congregation were urging him to drop out of school and serve the church full time. He believed their exaggerated compliments and made an appointment with the seminary registrar to drop out of school. But the registrar had faced this issue with students many times and was ready for him. He said, "My brother, the Lord has waited a long time for you to come along, and He can wait two more years until you graduate. You can serve the Lord as a good student just as much as you can by being a good pastor, and God can bless both." My friend wisely remained in school and, as far as I know, was grateful for the registrar's wise counsel.

As we wait on the Lord, it may seem to us a waste of time; but we must realize that the Lord is not only working *for* us but working *in* us. He wants us to be adequately prepared to do the work He is preparing for us (Phil. 1:6). If we start taking shortcuts and avoiding the necessary disciplines of the Christian life, we will not be able to fight the battles, carry the burdens, and glorify the Lord. The Lord avoided the shortcuts when He led His people out of Egypt (Exod. 13:17–22). Why? Because there were "faith lessons" for them to learn as He transformed them from a nation of slaves into the dedicated people of God. When Jesus was tempted by Satan (Matt. 4:1–11), the tempter suggested that He take the "easy way" and avoid the cross; but Jesus boldly rejected Satan's plan. The short cut is always rougher than the main highway. Today we live in a culture that seems to ignore personal discipline (unless you are an athlete) and emphasizes speed and pleasure. After all, having fun is more important than building faith or serving God. Or is it?

After Nathan the prophet shared God's gracious covenant with David, the king went and sat before the Lord, worshiped, and communed with Him (1 Chron. 17:16–27). As he considered the bountiful blessings the Lord had bestowed upon him, David could do nothing more. Mary of Bethany sat at Jesus' feet and listened to His word, and Jesus commended her for doing it (Luke 10:38–42). When life is pressing instead of blessing, it is time for us to get alone with the Lord, sit at His feet, and listen to His word as He teaches us and equips us for the work to come.

Yes, there are times when we must learn to sit still and let God equip us for the work He has chosen for us. We must say with David, "My times are in Your hand" (Ps. 31:15).

We Must Learn to Stand Still

"Do not be afraid. Stand still, and see the salvation of the LORD, which He will accomplish for you today" (Exod. 14:13). Moses spoke those heartening words to the children of Israel on the night they were released from Egyptian bondage. The Red Sea was before them, the Egyptian army was pursuing them, and there was no place to escape and hide. It looked like certain annihilation but for one thing: God was on the side of the Israelites! "If God is for us, who can be against us?" (Rom. 8:31). Moses shouted. "The LORD will fight for you and you shall hold your peace" (Exod. 14:14). The Israelites were to "be still" and "stand still" and trust God to do the rest. Moses lifted his rod and stretched out his hand,

and the Lord put a cloud of darkness between the army and the Israelites. Then He opened a dry road through the water, clear to the other side! When the Egyptians attempted to use that road to pursue the Israelites, the two walls of water crashed down upon them and the army was destroyed.

We find a similar victory recorded in 2 Chronicles 20. The Ammonites and Moabites with their allies attacked Jehoshaphat, king of Judah, and his people. Jehoshaphat urged the people to pray, and he set the example himself; and the Lord answered, speaking through Jehaziel the prophet. "Do not be afraid or dismayed by this great multitude, for the battle is not yours, but God's" (2 Chron. 20:15). The Lord defeated the invaders and brought glory to His name. "Then the realm of Jehoshaphat was quiet, for his God gave him rest all around" (2 Chron. 20:30).

"And this is the victory that has overcome the world — our faith" (1 John 5:4). But there are two kinds of battles in the Christian life: those the Lord helps us win and those He wins for us as we patiently wait. Through faith, we become conquerors as we defeat the enemy, but we can also become "more than conquerors" (Rom. 8:37) *by letting the enemy defeat himself!* If we always draw up our own battle plans and use our own weapons, then the Lord cannot fight for us; but if we turn it all over to Him and wait, He will win the victory. We must have wisdom to know when to fight for victory and when to wait for victory.

In the congregation of one of the churches I was privileged to serve was a small group of critical dissidents whose negative attitude poisoned the atmosphere of business meetings and created problems for my two of my predecessors. The Lord cautioned me to wait patiently and pray and not to depend on my own strategy, and He would solve the problem in His own way and at His own time. I prayed daily for these people and ministered to them just as I ministered to the other members. After five years, in one business meeting, the leader of the dissidents and his main helper were both removed from office by the officers of the church. I simply sat there and watched it all happen! Conquerors are always praised, but "more than conquerors" can only say, "Praise the Lord for what He has done!"

The American inventor Thomas A. Edison wisely said, "Everything comes to him who hustles while he waits." How do you hustle and wait at the same time? You are "on the move" inwardly, learning, trusting, and growing, but waiting outwardly for God to work out His plan. "Commit your way to the LORD, trust also in Him, and He shall bring it to pass.... Rest in the LORD, and wait patiently for Him" (Ps. 37:5, 7).

"Do not be afraid! Stand still and see the salvation of the LORD, which He will accomplish for you today" (Exod. 14:13).

We Must Learn to Lie Still

A night of healthy sleep is a gift from God, while a restless night can lead to a distressful day. "I lay down and slept," wrote David in Psalm 3:5; "I awoke, for the LORD sustained me." In the next psalm he wrote, "Meditate within your heart on your bed, and be still.... I will both lie down in peace, and sleep; for You alone, O LORD, make me dwell in safety" (vv. 4, 8). We are not sure whether Solomon wrote Psalm 127 or David wrote it for the education of his son, but verse 2 assures us that "He gives His beloved sleep."

It is not enough for us to learn to *be still* and *sit still* and *stand still*. We must also learn to *lie still* and experience the healing rest of heaven after a busy day. To toss and turn all night because something is bothering us is to rob ourselves of the blessings God wants to give us. "Be angry and do not sin" (Ps. 4:4) is quoted by Paul in Ephesians 4:26, and he was writing to Christian believers. Are we angry at ourselves, at a friend, at the Lord? Are we nurturing some irritation down inside that is poisoning our outlook on life? Paul added to his quotation of Psalm 4:4, "Do not let the sun go down on your wrath." In other words, be sure your heart is right or your attempts at sleep will go wrong.

The Lord can teach us at night. On the bed stand next to my pillow is a special light attached to a pad of paper. The light turns on noiselessly with a simple touch and focuses on the paper. Many times the Lord has awakened me and taken me to "night school" to meditate on His truth. He wants me to be like the "blessed man" of Psalm 1:2 and meditate on Scripture day and night, or the godly man who wrote in Psalm 119:148, "My eyes are awake through the night watches, that I may meditate on Your word." As I meditate and the Lord unfolds His truth, I write notes on the pad of paper, and the next morning I take them with me to my study and file them where they belong or write the notes in the margin of my study Bible.

I believe the Holy Spirit can work in the subconscious mind if we focus our minds on God's truth. When I was in high school, I did my homework in the evening and sometimes I would have difficulty with a geometry problem. I would "file it away" in my mind and go to bed, and frequently wake up in the morning with the solution to the problem in my mind! I assumed my subconscious mind had worked on it all night. This experience has been repeated many times when I was preparing sermons: the text I was pondering "came alive" when I woke up during the night or in the morning. Of course, we must "feed our minds" as we study and give the Spirit something to work with; otherwise there will be no sermon worth listening to and the congregation may go to sleep! Yes, the Lord can instruct us in the night seasons if we hide His word in our hearts and meditate on it (Ps. 16:7). This may not work for everybody, but it has certainly worked for me.

There is not only *schooling* at night but also *singing* "songs in the night" (Pss. 42:8; 77:6; Job 35:10). Anyone can sing during a sunny day, but to sing in the night is another matter. King David sang psalms in the night; Jesus sang after the last supper before He was arrested (Matt. 26:30); and Paul and Silas sang at night in the Philippian prison (Acts 16:25). When we find ourselves under a cloud or in the shadows, we can always praise the Lord with "psalms and hymns and spiritual songs" (Eph. 5:19). Soon the light will shine again. We can even "sing ourselves to sleep" as we lie on our bed and worship the Lord. If we go to sleep at night praising the Lord, we will wake up in the morning still in fellowship with Him.

As we meditate at night on the Lord and His truth, we may also have a time of *searching*. "You have tested my heart; You have visited me in the night; You have tried me and found nothing" (Ps. 17:3). In the stillness of the night, the Holy Spirit may remind us of things said and done — or *not* said and done — that need to be dealt with. My little light and pad of paper come in handy then and I can write myself a note to get things done! The prayer of Psalm 139:23–24 is just right as we wait for sleep to come.

I visited a hospital patient who said, "I just could not get to sleep last night. Then I remembered the verse that says God neither slumbers nor sleeps, and I decided it was foolish for both of us to stay awake — so I turned over and went to sleep." Do not waste time counting sheep. Instead, keep in touch with the Shepherd *who never goes to sleep!*

"For so He gives His beloved sleep" (Ps. 127:2).

7

We Must Lose Our Life to Save It

*And He began to teach them that the Son of Man must suffer
many things, and be rejected by the elders and chief priests and
scribes, and be killed, and after three days rise again. He spoke
this word openly. And Peter took Him aside and began to rebuke Him. But when He had turned around and looked at His
disciples, He rebuked Peter, saying, "Get behind Me, Satan! For
you are not mindful of the things of God, but the things of men."
When He had called the people to Himself, with His disciples, also,
He said to them, "Whoever desires to come after Me, let him deny
himself, and take up his cross, and follow Me. For whoever desires
to save his life will lose it, but whoever loses his life for My sake
and the gospel's will save it. For what will it profit a man if he
gains the whole world, and loses his own soul? Or what will a
man give in exchange for his own soul? For whoever is ashamed
of Me and My words in this adulterous and sinful generation, of
him the Son of Man also will be ashamed when He comes in the
glory of His Father with the holy angels." (Mark 8:31–38)*

*But Jesus answered them, saying, "The hour is come that the Son
of Man should be glorified. Most assuredly, I say to you, unless a
grain of wheat falls into the ground and dies, it remains alone;
but if it dies, it produces much grain. He who loves his life will*

> *lose it, and he who hates his life in this world will keep it for eternal life. If anyone serves Me, let him follow Me; and where I am, there My servant will be also. If anyone serves Me, him My Father will honor." (John 12:23–26)*

DURING OUR LORD'S THREE YEARS of ministry on earth, He not only taught the multitudes publicly, but He also taught His disciples privately and equipped them for the ministries they would have after He had returned to heaven. Jesus said to the Father, "I have manifested Your name to the men whom You have given Me out of the world. They were Yours, You gave them to Me, and they have kept Your word. . . . For I have given to them the words which You have given Me; and they have received them, and have known surely that I came forth from You; and they have believed that You sent Me" (John 17:6, 8). On the Day of Pentecost, He sent the Holy Spirit to teach them and enable them to recall what He had taught them (John 14:26; Acts 2). If we surrender to Him, that same Holy Spirit will teach us, remind us, and empower us so that we might bear witness of Him (Acts 1:8).

Our Lord's private teaching ministry reached a crucial point when Jesus revealed to the disciples that He was going to Jerusalem to die. On behalf of himself and the disciple band, Peter had affirmed his faith in Jesus, the Son of God, and from that time on, our Lord prepared him and the other disciples for Calvary (Matt. 16:13–26). As we study the stages in this "classroom experience" from Mark 8–9, we get a better understanding of the meaning of *true discipleship.*

An Ominous Announcement (Mark 8:31)

The time had come for Jesus to tell the apostles clearly that He was going to Jerusalem to die. The apostles had been given "metaphorical hints" of Christ's sacrificial death, but now the Master was clearly explaining it to them. John the Baptist had called Him "the Lamb of God" (John 1:29), which clearly speaks of sacrifice. And Jesus spoke of His "temple" being destroyed and built up again (John 2:13–22). He spoke to Nicodemus (and whomever else was present) about the serpent that Moses lifted up in the wilderness (John 3:14), and He compared Himself to the prophet Jonah, whose experience with the great fish pictures death, burial, and resurrection (Matt. 12:38–40). Jesus was heading for Jerusalem, because "it cannot be that a prophet should perish outside of Jerusalem" (Luke 13:33).

The apostles were learning slowly and painfully. They had attended the synagogue and the temple where the Scriptures were read and expounded, so they had heard the things pertaining to the Messiah (see Luke 24:13–35). But the priests and scribes did not have a clear understanding of the subject. The Old Testament speaks of both a suffering Messiah and a reigning Messiah, and the teachers could not explain this puzzling conflict between suffering and glory. Some pointed to Psalm 22 and Isaiah 53 and taught that there would be *two* Messiahs! Jesus made it clear to His apostles that He was the Messiah and that it was prophesied that He would be rejected by His people, suffer humiliation and pain, and finally die on the cross. First the suffering and then the glory, as Peter makes clear in his first epistle.

Christians today are prone to take the cross for granted, and many of them wear the cross as a piece of attractive jewelry. We see crosses on grave markers as well as on church buildings and in worship centers. How often have we nonchalantly sung about the cross while our minds were wandering miles away? After Jesus had spoken about the cross, James and John selfishly asked Him to give each of them *a throne* (Mark 10:32–40)! We wonder how many times the apostles had seen convicted criminals, each carrying his cross out to the place of execution. So humiliating and inhuman was crucifixion that it was not mentioned in polite company, and no one would have made a cross into a piece of jewelry any more than we today would the electric chair or the gallows. Jesus had declared what lay before Him and His disciples, and there was no denying it or escaping it. The Son of Man *must* be lifted up (John 3:14).

An Erroneous Rebuke (Mark 8:32–33)

Before we criticize Peter severely for his impetuous words (imagine telling God what to do!), we must remember that what he said was meant to be an expression of his love for Christ. He did not want Him to suffer and die. If any believers in their prayers, ministries, or conversations have never spoken carelessly as Peter did, let them cast the first stone. He was a young believer and still had much to learn; but he loved Jesus and could not understand why He had to die. Peter did not realize that Satan was using him to discourage Jesus from obeying His Father's will. (The word "rebuke" in v. 33 is the same word used in rebuking the demons in Mark 1:25 and 3:12.) "Save yourself" is the world's philosophy of life, but Jesus pointed out that "give yourself" is His philosophy of life. Jesus would have more to say to His disciples about the cross (9:30; 20:32–34), and what Peter wrote in his epistles about suffering and glory indicates that he learned his lesson.

Note that "Jesus turned" (the Greek is "turned sharply") and looked at the other disciples before He rebuked Peter (v. 33), because what He said to Peter applies to all of His followers. The basic question is, "Whose side are we on, God's or Satan's?" There must never be compromise. *Nobody is more dangerous to the work of God than a leader out of the will of God.* We see this demonstrated dramatically in the sins of Abraham, Jacob, Joshua, King Saul, and King David. When Satan succeeds in causing a leader to stumble and fall, he influences the lives of many people and robs God of glory.

Peter rebuked the Lord immediately after he had been blessed by Jesus for his confession of faith (Matt. 16:18–20). We must be especially careful in the high and holy experiences of the Christian life, for that is when Satan often attacks. "Therefore let him who thinks he stands take heed lest he fall" (1 Cor. 10:12). Peter made the same mistake on the Mount of Transformation (Matt. 17:1–5) and in the upper room (John 13:2–10). It was Peter who wrote, "Be sober, be vigilant; because your adversary the devil walks about like a roaring lion, seeking whom he may devour" (1 Peter 5:8).

We must learn to walk by faith, no matter what the circumstances are around us or the feelings within us. Both may be deceptive and motivate us to do the wrong thing. Peter was sure he could die for the Lord, yet he went to sleep in the garden and later denied the Lord three times (Luke 22:31–34). "The heart is deceitful above all things, and desperately wicked; who can know it?" (Jer. 17:9). We may think we are directed by the Spirit, but we might be deceived by the spirits! "Beloved, do not believe every spirit, but test the spirits, whether they are of God" (1 John 4:1). We must pray, walk in the Spirit, and feed on the word of God so that we always have the discernment to detect the devil's counterfeit offers. We need discernment from the Lord, for the enemy is a skillful deceiver.

A Serious Decision (Mark 8:34–37)

Life is a precious gift from God, and we can do three things with that gift. We can *waste* our lives having a "good time" and one day come to the end only to discover we had not really lived. Or we can *spend* our lives, living comfortably like our friends and neighbors but lacking purpose and the blessing of God. We live only to please ourselves. We might leave something behind, but we have not sent anything ahead. Our choice must be to *invest* our lives, to give everything to the Lord, follow Him in everything, and let Him determine the dividends. This kind of life is called "discipleship." It is what Jesus meant when He said to the disciples and the crowd, "Whoever desires to come after Me, let him deny himself, and take up his cross, and follow Me. For whoever desires to save his life will lose it. but whoever loses his life for My sake and the gospel's will save it" (Mark 8:34–35).

Luke 9:57–62 presents three potential disciples, two who offered themselves to Jesus and one who was called by Jesus. And all three failed.

> Now it happened as they journeyed on the road, that someone said to Him, "Lord, I will follow You wherever You go." And Jesus said to him, "Foxes have holes and birds of the air have nests, but the Son of Man has nowhere to lay His head." Then He said to another, "Follow Me." But he said, "Lord, let me first go and bury my father." Jesus said to him, "Let the dead bury their own dead, but you go and preach the kingdom of God." And another also said, "Lord, I will follow you, but let me first go and bid them farewell who are at my house." But Jesus said to him, "No one, having put his hand to the plow, and looking back, is fit for the kingdom of God."

The phrase "me first" shows up twice in this narrative (vv. 59, 61), but "me first" should never be on the lips or in the mind of a true disciple. It must be "Jesus first." Here's how Jesus describes a disciple in Mark 8:34: "Whoever desires to come after Me, let him deny himself, and take up his cross, and follow Me."

None of the three men involved in this episode really understood discipleship. The first one wanted assured comfort, but disciples must deny themselves. The second man wanted to wait for his father to die, but *the son was supposed to take up his cross and die daily!* The third man wanted to enjoy a farewell party, something he could look back upon with good memories. But true disciples do not look back; they look ahead and follow Jesus.

Our Lord's message is clear: every believer is not called into "full-time Christian service," but every believer *is* called into full-time Christian living, *which is discipleship*. It is important to notice the tenses of the verbs in Mark 8:34: we deny ourselves once and for all (Rom. 12:1–2); we take up our cross once and for all (Gal. 2:20); we follow Him obediently and never look back. If like the three would-be disciples, we pamper ourselves and try to save ourselves, we lose our lives and will never have an opportunity to live them again. Jesus said, "For whoever desires to save his life will lose it, but whoever loses his life for My sake and the gospel's will save it" (Mark 8:35).

Our Lord does not tell us to deny this thing or that thing but to deny ourselves. That takes care of everything! He does not give me a crown and make me a celebrity, but He does give me a cross and make me a living sacrifice and a laboring servant (Rom. 12:1–2). To live for myself and gain the whole world with its wealth, pleasures, and honors is to lose everything! When a famine occurred in Canaan, Abraham disobeyed the Lord and escaped to Egypt, taking his nephew Lot with him. And that was the beginning of Lot's gaining the world but losing his life (Gen. 12:10–13:13). Once he had a taste of Egypt (the world), he started walking by sight and not by faith and measuring everything by Egypt. The result was tragedy for Lot and his family (Gen. 19).

Jesus said, "I have come that they may have life, and that they may have it more abundantly" (John 10:10). In order to give us life, He gave His own life on the cross. And now He asks that we give our lives to Him so that others may hear the message of eternal life. We give ourselves to Jesus for His sake and for the sake of sinners who do not know the gospel. This is the paradox of the victorious and fruitful Christian life: we lose our lives to gain His life and we share our lives that others may know Him. It for His sake and the sake of the gospel (Mark 8:35).

A Glorious Future (Mark 8:38–9:8)

After our Lord had taught His disciples about the cross, He immediately moved into a lesson about His future glorious kingdom and the glory they would share. In the Christian life, suffering and glory go together. I have often seen a plaque in Christian homes that reads, "No cross, no crown." Jesus demonstrated that simple statement when He took Peter, James, and John to the Mount of Transfiguration where the Father revealed the Son's glory and the glory of the coming kingdom.

It is interesting to note that Jesus involved these three disciples in the same three experiences: the transfiguration (Mark 9:1–13), the raising of Jairus' daughter from the dead (Mark 5:21–43), and our Lord's prayer of agony in the garden of Gethsemane (Mark 14:32–42). These three events remind me of Philippians 3:10: "that I may know Him [the transfiguration] and the power of His resurrection [raising Jairus' daughter], and the fellowship of His sufferings [in the garden with Jesus]."

When our Lord first taught His disciples that He would give His life on the cross, Peter opposed him and was rebuked by Jesus. "Get behind Me, Satan!" (Mark 8:33). The title "Satan" means "adversary, enemy." But Peter was a chosen apostle! Yes he was, but when the children of God oppose the will of God and live like the world, they become the enemies of God! Paul gave the Philippian believers an admonition about this. "Brethren, join in following my example, and not those who so walk, as you have us for a pattern. For many walk, of whom I have told you often, and now tell you even weeping, that they are the enemies of the cross of Christ: whose end is destruction, whose God is their belly, and whose glory is in their shame — who set their mind on earthly things" (Phil. 3:17–19). He was writing about professed Christians *in the churches!* Sad to say, they are still with us. Jesus made it clear that following Him meant being despised and hated by the world and even by worldly Christians.

The apostle Peter laid hold of the truth that obedient suffering ultimately leads to glory.

Jesus told him that one day he would stretch out his hands and be crucified (John 21:18–19); and when it did happen, Peter knew there was glory awaiting him, just as it awaited Jesus when He was crucified (1 Peter 1:11, 21). The believers to whom Peter sent his first epistle were assured that their impending persecution would lead to eternal glory (1 Peter 4:12–19; 5:1–4). Peter urged them to lead godly lives so that they might glorify Jesus and bear witness to unbelievers.

Our Lord never taught that the Christian life was easy, comfortable, and without dangers. I have heard that kind of preaching from the "health and wealth" evangelists and have rejected it because Jesus taught just the opposite! "In the world you will have tribulation; but be of good cheer, I have overcome the world" (John 16:33; see Matt. 5:10–12; 10:16–26; Rom. 8:17, 35–39; John 15:18–27). If we suffer because we have done wrong, we deserve it; but if we suffer for doing good and standing for the right, that is another matter (1 Peter 3:13–4:19).

I once saw a poster that read, "If Jesus is your Lord, then the future is your friend." Our suffering for Christ today means glory with Him in the future. *Our Savior's wounds from Calvary are today glorified in heaven!* If we have been faithful, we will one day see our own scars transformed into radiance to the glory of God.

We must lose our life if we would save it.

But if we save it for ourselves, we will lose it.

Have we counted the cost?

8

When Light Becomes Darkness

Do not lay up for yourselves treasures on earth, where moth and rust destroy and where thieves break in and steal; but lay up for yourselves treasures in heaven, where neither moth nor rust destroys and where thieves do not break in and steal. For where your treasure is, there your heart will be also. If therefore your eye is good, your whole body will be full of light. But if your eye is bad, your whole body will be full of darkness. If therefore the light that is in you is darkness, how great is that darkness! No one can serve two masters: for either he will hate the one and love the other, or else he will be loyal to the one and despise the other. You cannot serve God and mammon. (Matt. 6:19–24)

For you were once darkness, but now you are light in the Lord. . . . And have no fellowship with the unfruitful works of darkness, but rather expose them. (Eph. 5:8, 11)

Do all things without complaining and disputing, that you may become blameless and harmless, children of God without fault in the midst of a crooked and perverse generation, among whom you shine as lights in the world. (Phil. 2:14–15)

OUR WORLD TODAY claims to be basking in the sunshine of unprecedented enlightenment, but I have my doubts that this assessment is true. I confess that enlightenment has been great in some areas of science, medicine, and communications, but I fear we are plunging more and more into darkness when it comes to obeying the law, respecting human rights, exercising wisdom, building character, and learning to love and serve one another to the glory of God.

To obtain these blessings we need the help of the Lord, but unfortunately God has officially been removed from the availability list. The major goal in life today seems to be increased enjoyment rather than developing moral and spiritual enlightenment and enrichment. I think we are living in a culture of darkness that is growing darker every day. There are more than two hundred references to darkness in the Bible, not just physical darkness but also a satanic darkness that controls both the minds and hearts of unbelievers and attacks the lives and ministries of believers.

The thickest darkness I have ever experienced was deep in the Mammoth Cave in Kentucky. Our guide warned us that the lights would be turned off briefly and that we must not move from our places. When the lights went out, you can be sure we obeyed! It gave me some idea of what the Egyptians experienced when God punished them with three days of thick darkness (Exod. 10:21–29). But that kind of darkness is only the absence of light. The spiritual darkness described in the Bible is a powerful force of its own, signifying the presence and work of the devil (Luke 22:53). "For we do not wrestle against flesh and blood, but against principalities, against powers, against the rulers of the darkness of this age, against spiritual hosts of wickedness in the heavenly places" (Eph. 6:12). That is a sobering sentence.

What are the essentials for God's people that they might be able to overcome the hosts of darkness in today's "enlightened" world?

We Must Surrender Ourselves Wholly to the Lord

The word "body" is used seven times in the Sermon on the Mount (Matt. 5:29–30; 6:22, 23, 25), because what we do with our body will either glorify the Lord or disgrace the name of Jesus (Matt. 5:13–20). I want to focus on Matthew 6:22–23. (See page 70 of quotations.) The believer's body is God's temple, indwelt by the Holy Spirit (1 Cor. 6:19–20). Jesus purchased our body by the shedding of His blood on the cross, and He wants us so to live that we will always glorify God. Jesus warned His hearers not to cultivate the kind of righteousness practiced by the scribes and Pharisees (Matt. 5:20). They had a form of righteousness that did not come from the heart nor did it glorify God. Outwardly, they seemed very religious, but inwardly they lacked the life and love of God. In Matthew 23, Jesus called them "hypocrites" (play actors) and denounced their religious practices. Since the believer's body is God's temple, we must avoid hypocrisy and live godly lives that glorify Him.

Romans 12:1–2 are familiar verses that instruct us to give the Lord our body, mind, and will and serve Him as "living sacrifices" that are acceptable to God. We cannot serve two masters (Matt. 6:24); Jesus alone must be our Lord. "But why do you call Me 'Lord, Lord' and do not do the things which I say?" (Luke 6:46). God's commandments are not burdens to bear but blessings to share and opportunities to glorify God as we minister to others.

The believer's body is not only God's temple, it is also His tool. He wants to use the members of our body as "instruments of righteousness to God" (Rom. 6:13–14). We were born with certain skills and when we were born again, we were given spiritual gifts to match those skills (1 Cor. 12). I was born with an inquisitive mind and a love for books and reading. When I was saved, I received a gift of teaching, and that has been my ministry all these years.

All believers must discover what gift or gifts they possess and use them for the building of the church. What makes us successful servants of God is not our talents or even our training, as important as they are, but our submission and obedience to the Lord and our dependence on the power of the Holy Spirit.

The believer's body is God's temple and tool, but it is also His treasury. "But we have this treasure [the gospel] in earthen vessels, that the excellence of the power might be of God and not of us" (2 Cor. 4:7). Our bodies were formed of the dust of the ground (Gen. 2:7), and yet the Holy Spirit of God is willing to dwell within us and enable us to share the word with others. God alone must receive the glory! It is immaterial that we are *earthen* vessels, for the main thing is that we hide God's word in our heart, cooperate with the Spirit, and keep our vessel clean. To defile the body is to sin against the Lord, grieve the Spirit, and lose the power of God.

We Must Have a "Good Eye"

Our key verses are Matthew 6:22–23: "The lamp of the body is the eye. If therefore your eye is good, your whole body will be full of light. But if your eye is bad, your whole body will be full of darkness. If therefore the light that is in you is darkness, how great is that darkness!" The paradox here is that the lost world thinks it is enlightened and that Christians are in the dark when it is the world that is in the dark and the Christians who have the light. When I trusted Jesus Christ as my Lord and Savior, my darkness was replaced by light and much of the so-called light in the world proved to be darkness.

Outlook always determines outcome. Eve looked at the forbidden tree, desired the fruit, ate it, shared it with her husband, and with Adam was punished by the Lord (Gen. 3:1–7). Lot looked at the plains of Jordan, chose them for his home, and ended up losing everything (Gen. 13:10; 19). King David looked lustfully upon his neighbor's wife and paid dearly for the sins that followed (2 Sam. 11–12). The eyes see, the mind imagines, the heart desires, and the will acts. James 1:12–18 pictures temptation and sin as a kind of pregnancy (see also Job 15:35; Ps. 7:14; Isa. 33:11; 59:4, 13). To give birth to sin day after day is a sad way to live.

The world looks at believers and concludes that they are "in the dark" or "living in the dark ages"; but actually it is the *un*-believers who are "in the dark." Spiritually minded believers see things as they really are. God's people who have healthy spiritual vision do not attempt to look two ways at the same time, serving two masters (Matt. 6:24) and being double-minded (James 1:6–8; 4:7–10). A divided eye gives you a twisted view of life, while the single (healthy) eye enables you to see matters as they really are. If you are walking with the Lord, you can depend on "the eyes of your heart" (Eph. 1:18, margin) to show you the truth. When it comes to spiritual things, unconverted people see darkness, but God's children see the light of the Lord and His truth.

The theme of light and darkness and spiritual discernment permeates the Gospel of John.

Often when Jesus spoke about spiritual matters, the unconverted listeners interpreted them literally as material matters. "And the light shines in the darkness, and the darkness did not comprehend it" (John 1:5). There were times when even our Lord's followers were in the dark! For example, in John 2:18–21, Jesus spoke of His death and resurrection, but the people thought He was speaking about destroying and rebuilding the temple in Jerusalem. In chapter 3, Nicodemus could not understand spiritual birth (v. 9), and the Samaritan woman in chapter 4 confused the "water of life" and the material water from Jacob's well (4:11–12). In that same chapter, when Jesus spoke to His disciples about the will of God, they thought He meant literal food (vv. 31–38). Our

Lord's message about His people eating His flesh and drinking His blood was taken literally by the Jewish crowd (6:41–58), and so were His references to heaven (7:32–36; 8:21–22). When He spoke about freedom, the listeners misinterpreted it (8:31–36). Jesus compared death to sleep, but the apostles did not understand the image (11:11–13), and Martha was confused about the resurrection (11:20–27).

Jesus is the light of the world (8:12), but unbelievers love the darkness and hate the light (John 3:19–21). They think that they have the light when they are actually living in spiritual darkness. John the Baptist pointed out Jesus to the crowd (John 1:29) because John was sent "to bear witness to the light" (1:6–9). *The only person you must tell that the light is shining is a blind person!* John's congregation was spiritually blind, especially the religious leaders. But we as followers of Jesus Christ must keep our spiritual eyesight healthy. We must know the Scriptures (Pss. 19:8; 119: 105, 130; Prov. 6:23); otherwise, the eyes of our heart will weaken. "Woe to those who call evil good and good evil; who put darkness for light, and light for darkness; who put bitter for sweet and sweet for bitter. Woe to those who are wise in their own eyes, and prudent in their own sight!" (Isa. 5:20–21).

When it comes to spiritual knowledge, the eyes of unbelievers are blind; but believers have spiritual vision that must be carefully maintained. "For with You is the fountain of life; in Your light we see light" (Ps. 36:9). God is light (1 John 1:5), Jesus the Son of God is light (John 8:12), and so are the Spirit of God (Rev. 4:5) and the word of God (Ps. 119:105). If we are acquainted with these divine lights, they can help us to understand other lights better — the light of nature, the light of history, and even the light of literature. During my years as a young student, my knowledge of Scripture enabled me to get more out of my studies, including history, fine arts, and literature. For example, when I opened *Moby Dick* and read the first line — "Call me Ishmael" — I was right at home!

But the Holy Spirit will also use the light of Scriptures to teach us about the people and circumstances we encounter — *and about ourselves*. As I study the past, my heavenly Father wants me to see truths as well as facts, character as well as conduct, and convictions as well as opinions. As G. Campbell Morgan used to say, "History is His story."

Jesus warned against double vision. He knew the tendency of people to want more of what the world has to offer while at the same time trying to keep their eyes on Jesus. We are so influenced by our current culture that we measure success by how much we earn and own rather than how much we have grown in the Lord. Covetousness is an especially dangerous sin. We boast that we own "things" when actually the things probably own us. If the things we own are used to serve others and honor the Lord, then we are laying up treasures in heaven; but if all we do is major in "keeping up appearances" to impress people, then we are laying up our treasures on earth and forfeiting the true treasures of the Lord.

Worry is one of the symptoms of covetousness (Matt. 6:23–34). Why? Because treasures on earth may be stolen or suffer decay, while treasures used to serve God are safely recorded in heaven. I read about a dedicated believer who gave a large sum of money to a Christian college, only to lose an almost equivalent sum months later because of unexpected worldwide economic reverses. "Too bad you gave away all that money," said a friend. "Oh, no!" said the businessman. "I gave that money to the Lord, and that's the money I still have, and it's safe!"

According to Colossians 3:5 covetousness is idolatry — putting our faith and hope in the material instead of the spiritual and doing it for ourselves and not for the Lord. If we want an inheritance in heaven, we must start now using our wealth for the glory of God (Matt. 6:19–21). "Command those who are rich in this present age not to be haughty, nor to trust in uncertain riches but in the living God, who gives us all things richly to enjoy" (1 Tim. 6:17). People who are always desiring more "things" are rarely satisfied (Eccl. 4:8). It is not wicked to save money (1 Tim. 5:8) or to possess things, but it is wicked when things possess us. "For the love of money is a root of all kinds of evil" (1 Tim. 6:10). When our Lord saw the rich young ruler reject everlasting life, He became very sorrowful. He said, "How hard it is for those who have riches to enter the kingdom of God!" (Luke 18:24). His disciples were astonished at what He said and they asked, "Who then can be saved?" The Jews in that day believed that anybody having great wealth was especially blessed of God, but Jesus taught otherwise (Luke 6:20–26; 12:15).

We Must Have a Heart That Seeks God

Jesus tells us what the people of the world are seeking. "Therefore do not worry, saying, 'What shall we eat? What shall we drink? What shall we wear?' For after all these things the Gentiles [unbelievers] seek. For your heavenly Father knows that you need these things. But seek first the kingdom of God and His righteousness, and all these things shall be added to you" (Matt. 6:31–33). Many of the advertisements in magazines and newspapers and on television and radio emphasize buying things and building your life on things, and there is nothing essentially wrong with possessing and enjoying things. But Jesus considers things to be "extra dividends" that the Father gives to those who put Him and His kingdom first in their life. The people who live only for things are robbing themselves of greater blessings: the righteousness of God and the rule of God in their lives. People who live for things do a great deal of worrying, while believers who put God first and live to expand His kingdom have confidence that God will meet all their needs (Phil. 4:19).

We receive God's righteousness and enter His kingdom when we trust Jesus Christ as our Savior and Lord (2 Cor. 5:16–21), and we grow in godliness and usefulness as we obey Him and encourage the lost to receive Christ. Our simple prayer "Your kingdom come" refers essentially to the return of Christ, but it also reminds us that He wants to share His kingdom *today* in homes, schools, offices, hospitals, and the halls of government. Wherever a dedicated believer is, the kingdom of God is there. When we put Christ first and obey Him, this enables the Holy Spirit to work in and through us as we walk in the Spirit. When Paul was in the prison in Philippi, God's kingdom was there and God cared for him (Acts 16:16–34), and likewise when he was on a ship in a terrible storm (Acts 27). When Paul was a prisoner in Rome, he wrote to Timothy, "At my first defense no one stood with me, but all forsook me. . . . But the Lord stood with me and strengthened me" (2 Tim. 4:16–17). The emperor was against Paul but the King of kings was for him!

The world seeks things and is worried and dissatisfied, while believers who put Jesus Christ first have all they need. The future of God's people means eternal light in heaven (Rev. 22:5), but for unbelievers the future means eternal "outer darkness" (Matt. 8:10–12; 22:13; 25:30). Unbelievers think God's people are in the dark and need to get smart, but it is the unbelievers who need to see the light and trust Jesus, the light of the world (John 8:12). Jesus said, "I have come as a light into the world, that whoever believes in Me should not abide in darkness" (John 12:46).

Unknown, and Yet Well Known

. . . as unknown, and yet well known. (2 Cor. 6:9)

And when Saul [Paul] had come to Jerusalem, he tried to join the disciples; but they were all afraid of him, and did not believe that he was a disciple. But Barnabas took him and brought him to the disciples. And he declared to them how he had seen the Lord on the road, and that He had spoken to him, and how he had preached boldly at Damascus in the name of Jesus. So he was with them at Jerusalem, coming in and going out. (Acts 9:26–28)

For the ways of man are before the eyes of the LORD, and He ponders all his paths. (Prov. 5:21)

The eyes of the LORD are in every place, keeping watch on the evil and the good. (Prov. 15:3)

Now while Paul waited for them at Athens, his spirit was provoked within him when he saw that the city was given over to idols. Therefore he reasoned in the synagogue with the Jews and with the Gentile worshipers, and in the marketplace daily with those who happened to be there. Then certain Epicurean and Stoic philosophers encountered him. And some said, "What does this babbler want to say?" Others said, "He seems to be a proclaimer

of foreign gods," because he preached to them Jesus and the resur-
rection. (Acts 17:16–18)

Behold what manner of love the Father has bestowed on us, that
we should be called children of God! Therefore the world does not
know us, because it did not know Him. (1 John 3:1)

But Jesus did not commit Himself to them, because He knew all
men, and had no need that anyone should testify of man, for He
knew what was in man. (John 2:24–25)

And there is no creature hidden from His sight, but all things are
naked and open to the eyes of Him to whom we must give ac-
count. (Heb. 4:13)

THE QUOTATION ON ONE of my favorite coffee mugs reads, "Reputation is made in a moment; character is built in a lifetime." There was not enough room on the mug to tell me who said it, but whoever it was certainly spoke the truth. The American writer Elbert Hubbard agreed with the unknown author when he wrote, "Many a man's reputation would not know his character if they met on the street."

There are people in history whose reputations are known by millions, but whose personal characters few people would want to imitate. There are also people whose characters are pure but their reputations have been tarnished by envious and hateful enemies who are good at telling lies. The apostle Paul was in that second category and so was our Lord Jesus Christ. Our Lord's enemies accused Him of being demonized and even called Him a gluttonous man and a winebibber (Matt. 11:18–19).

The congregation in Corinth was divided four ways because not everybody had the same opinion of Paul's character and ministry (1 Cor. 1:10–17). Some questioned his apostolic authority while others accused him of using his ministry for personal gain. In his letters, Paul defended himself and lovingly pointed out to them the many ways the church had failed to obey the will of God. The Corinthian Christians claimed to know all about Paul but they really did not know him well at all, so he proceeded to tell them in his letter the dangers and difficulties he had experienced for their sake (2 Cor. 11–12). Paul was not a famous celebrity, nor did he want to be. Paul was a faithful servant, "as unknown, and yet well-known" (9:6). In the history of the church, you find the names of many famous men and women who, like Paul, served and suffered and yet were ignored or criticized by the very people for whom they gave their best.

As I meditated on this paradox — "as unknown, and yet well-known" — I found myself asking three questions.

Do We Really Know Other People?

During the sixty years plus of our ministry, my wife and I have met many people, not only in the United States but also in other countries. Some of these people we have come to know very well, while others are acquaintances we touch base with from time to time. You must travel with people and spend time with them in their homes if you want to move from acquaintanceship into a deepening friendship. Paul spent eighteen months ministering in Corinth during his first visit, and while this does not match his nearly three years in Ephesus, it was time enough to learn to love the people and carry them away in his heart.

However, some of the Corinthians did not take Paul into their hearts, and this created serious problems. In his first letter to the Corinthian believers, Paul said that God had made him and the other apostles "a spectacle to the world" (4:9). The word translated "spectacle" (*theatron* in the Greek text) gives us the English word "theater." In other words, these people considered Paul to be just an actor playing a part. But that would make him a hypocrite, a word that comes from the Greek and means "play actor." There were people in Paul's day who were not sincere in their Christian testimony but were only playing a part (2 Cor. 11:5–15), but Paul was certainly not among them. In my own experience, I have worked alongside people who turned out to be pretenders and eventually imitated Demas and went back into the world (2 Tim. 4:10).

Occasionally Paul was not identified accurately. Even Christ's apostles did not recognize Paul as one of their number and were afraid of him, but Barnabas defended him and they changed their minds (Acts 9:26–30). The Greek scholars in Athens thought he was a confused visiting philosopher (Acts 17:18–20), and the Roman soldiers thought he was an escaped Egyptian criminal (Acts 21:37–39). The Roman governor Festus knew next to nothing about him and admitted it (Acts 25:13–27). But the demons recognized Paul (Acts 19:11–15)! And yet, in all his ministry, Paul had never used deception but had always been honest and without guile in his ministry (2 Cor. 6:1–10).

How can we verify potential church members or staff members to be sure they are born again (2 Peter 2:1–3)? The apostle John in his first epistle gives us a number of inspired "birthmarks" of true believers, beginning with obedience to the Lord's commandments (2:1–6). True believers have love for the people of God (2:7–11) and live a consistent Christian life (2:12–14). They are separated from the world (2:15–17), faithful to God's people and God's word (2:18–23). We must seek the guidance of the Holy Spirit (2:20, 27), lest we carelessly allow the "antichrist crowd" to start infecting the church (2:18–19). In the parable of the tares, Jesus warns us that Satan is a counterfeiter and sows counterfeit Christians wherever Jesus sows true believers (Matt. 13:24–30, 36–43); and Paul teaches the same thing (2 Cor. 11:13–15). We must ask God for humility and wisdom (James 1:5) and take heed to Matthew 7:1–6, or we might not really come to know the people we are trying to serve. If you have ever been misunderstood, you know how painful it can be.

Jesus knows what is in every person (John 2:23–25). He knew who Peter was and what he would become (John 1:42; 21:17–19), and He also knew Nathanael (John 1:43–51). He could read the hearts and minds of the crowds (John 5:38–47; 6:60–66) and critics (Matt. 9:4; 12:25). He knew that Judas was a traitor (John 6:67–71; 13:11). King David warned his son Solomon that "the LORD searches all hearts and understands all the intent of the thoughts" (1 Chron. 28:9); he also wrote that God "knows the secrets of the heart" (Pss. 44:21; 139:1–6). "The heart is deceitful above all things, and desperately wicked; who can know it?" (Jer. 17:9). The apostle John warned the churches of his day and today, "And all the churches shall know that I am He who searches the minds and the hearts" (Rev. 2:23).

The older I have grown in the things of the Lord, the more understanding and forgiving I have become regarding those who have attacked me or differed from me. I do not think I am compromising, but I do believe that the Lord is enabling me to practice that love which "is not provoked" but "bears all things" (1 Cor. 13:5, 7). Today I find it far easier to call others "Christians" who are not in my so-called camp, and I hope they feel the same way about me.

Do We Really Know Ourselves?

Psychologists tell us that childhood is a time for pretending, but maturity demands that we be authentic and not wear masks. Maturity can only be developed from reality. In Matthew 23, Jesus accused the Pharisees of being hypocrites. The meaning of the

Greek word translated "hypocrite" is "play actor," for ancient Greek players wore masks to depict their various parts in the play. This does not mean that we cannot fulfill several adult roles during the day — parent, sibling, employee, friend, and neighbor — but we must always be the same person no matter what our roles might be. Being true to ourselves unifies our lives, but once our false self appears, we become double-minded and this brings instability (James 1:8). We may briefly impress others, but we are not building the kind of mature character that honors the Lord and leads to a fruitful Christian life.

Many people are ignorant of their own potential, what the Lord can make out of them and accomplish through them. Moses argued with the Lord that he was not qualified to lead Israel (Exod. 3–4), yet see what he accomplished by saying yes to God. Gideon was sure that he and his family were losers, but God transformed him into a courageous general (Judg. 6–7). The young prophet Jeremiah felt unprepared for his ministry, but what a servant he turned out to be (Jer. 1)!

But there also lurks in us the potential for failure if we are not honest with ourselves. King Saul had impressive physical stature and great popularity, but his envy, pride, and gradual spiritual decay brought him defeat and death. The apostle Peter was a brave man who was sure he could die for Jesus. Yet he slept when he should have been praying, attacked when he should have been obeying, and followed when he should have fled away. But keep in mind that *all* the apostles echoed Peter's boast, so they were guilty too (Matt. 26:31–35).

The scribes and Pharisees were guilty of cultivating a false self that kept them from receiving God's truth. They refused to face themselves honestly and submit to the will of the Lord.

How do we get acquainted with ourselves? By paying attention to the Lord's teaching and submitting to His testing, which Hebrews 12:1–11 calls chastening. Satan tempts us to bring out the *worst* in us, but the Lord tests us to bring out the *best* in us. When God chastens us, it is not a judge punishing criminals but a loving Father helping His children discover themselves and develop themselves. David experienced much testing from the Lord, but his faith and obedience turned the shepherd boy into a victorious soldier and a successful king.

As brothers and sisters in God's family, we can help one another discover our strengths and overcome our weaknesses. I thank God for family, friends, and co-laborers who have helped me better understand myself and my work. "Faithful are the wounds of a friend, but the kisses of an enemy are deceitful" (Prov. 27:6). We must look at ourselves in the mirror of God's word (James 1:21–27) and ask God to deal with our weaknesses and protect our strengths. We must confess our sins to the Lord (1 John 1:9) and "wash" in the water of the word (Eph. 5:26). Experiencing God's forgiveness is a humbling experience that reassures us that we belong to Him and that He loves us.

Do We Really Know the Lord?

The nation of Israel in the Old Testament was frequently guilty of spiritual blindness, a lack of understanding of the heart and mind of their great God. They heard His words and saw His wonders and yet deliberately disobeyed His will, sometimes tempting God and sometimes deliberately rebelling. But when I read the four Gospels, I am reminded that the twelve apostles did not always understand the character, power, and works of Jesus. Sometimes they made suggestions that were outrageous. But before we denounce either Israel or the apostles, we should review church history and admit that our forefathers were not always obedient, nor are we.

The twelve apostles had the privilege of living with Jesus, hearing His words, and seeing His works, and yet many times they did not really know Him. They scolded a man who was casting out demons in the name of Jesus (Mark 9:38–41). They tried to prevent parents from bringing their children to Jesus (Mark 10:13–16). James and John wanted to call fire down from heaven to destroy an unfriendly Samaritan village (Luke 9:51–56). They told Jesus to dismiss a hungry crowd so the people could find food (Matt. 14:15), and they also wanted Him to get rid of a burdened Gentile woman who was pestering them (Matt. 15:22–28). Jesus told His disciples He would be crucified in Jerusalem and Peter took Him aside and reprimanded Him (Matt. 16:21–23). No wonder Jesus cried out one day, "How long should I bear with you?" (Matt. 17:17)!

God wants us to know Him personally, for to know Him is to love Him, and to love Him is to worship Him and obey Him. As we are "increasing in the knowledge of God" (Col. 1:10), we are also receiving the grace and peace we need to serve Him day by day (2 Peter 1:2). God's light has shone in our hearts and has brought to us "the knowledge of the glory of God in the face of Jesus Christ" (2 Cor. 4:6). We will have all eternity to grow in our knowledge of God, but we must begin learning and growing today. Paul said that his greatest desire was to "know Him and the power of His resurrection, and the fellowship of His sufferings, being conformed to His death" (Phil. 3:10). Paul makes it clear in this verse that before believers begin to conform to Christ in His life and death, they must have a *personal* experience of knowing Christ, a *powerful* experience of His resurrection victory, and at times a *painful* experience of suffering for His sake. But ultimately this leads to our becoming more and more conformed to His image and not conformed to this world (Rom. 8:29; 12:1–2).

God wants us to know His will (Acts 22:14), understand His will (Eph. 5:17), delight in His will (Ps. 40:8), and obey His will from our heart (Eph. 6:6). He has given us the Spirit of God, the word of God, and the church of the living God to encourage and enable us. He is the God of all grace (1 Peter 5:10), the living God (Ps. 42:2), the merciful God (Exod. 34:6), the almighty God (Rev. 1:8; 4:8), the holy God (Ps. 99:9), the God of love and peace (2 Cor.13:11), the God of patience and comfort (Rom. 15:4), and we are privileged to call Him "our God" (1 Cor. 6:11) and "my God" (Phil. 4:19).

Jesus came to reveal the Father to us. "If you had known Me," He told the disciples, "you would have known My Father" (John 14:7). The unconverted people we witness to point only to the Old Testament and argue that our God is a bully who destroys cities and kills innocent people. If these unbelievers could understand theology, I would answer their worn-out arguments, but instead, I simply point them to Jesus. See Him! God carrying a baby in His arms! God touching and healing a leper! God giving sight to a blind man! God feeding thousands of hungry people! *God dying on a cross for the sins of the world!* Does that look like a hard-hearted bully?

Like Jesus and Paul, every faithful Christian will be "as unknown, and yet well-known."

They will encounter envious criticism and unfair accusations, but like Jesus and Paul they will go on with life and ministry and seek only to serve the Lord and glorify Him. The only words we should strive to hear are, "Well done, good and faithful servant; you were faithful over a few things, I will make you ruler over many things. Enter into the joy of your Lord" (Matt. 25:21).

This paragraph from a sermon by the gifted Scottish preacher George H. Morrison has encouraged me:

If, then, you are truly following Christ, never be anxious to explain yourself; do not be eager to be understood, and never grow feverish to be understood. Take up thy cross; study to be quiet; redeem the time; follow the gleam bravely. Remember that with all the saints you are to walk heavenward as one unknown.[1]

1   George H. Morrison, *The Unlighted Luster* (London: Hodder and Stoughton, n.d.), 274–75.

10

Sorrowing Yet Always Rejoicing

Those who sow in tears shall reap in joy. He who continually goes forth weeping, bearing seed for sowing, shall doubtless come again with rejoicing, bringing his sheaves with him. (Ps. 126:5–6)

How long shall I take counsel in my soul, having sorrow in my heart daily? (Ps. 13:2)

The pains of death surrounded me, and the pangs of Sheol laid hold of me; I found trouble and sorrow. (Ps. 116:3)

Though He causes grief, yet He will show compassion, according to the multitude of His mercies. (Lam. 3:32)

Do not sorrow, for the joy of the LORD is your strength. (Neh. 8:10)

These things I have spoken to you, that My joy may remain in you, and that your joy may be full. (John 15:11)

A woman, when she is in labor, has sorrow because her hour has come; but as soon as she has given birth to the child, she no longer remembers the anguish, for joy that a human being has been born into the world. Therefore you now have sorrow; but I will see you again and your heart will rejoice, and your joy no one will take from you. (John 16:21–22)

. . . rejoicing in hope, patient in tribulation, continuing steadfastly in prayer. (Rom. 12:12)

. . . as sorrowful, yet always rejoicing. (2 Cor. 6:10)

Rejoice in the Lord always. Again I will say, rejoice! (Phil. 4:4)

"AS SORROWFUL, YET ALWAYS REJOICING" is a challenging paradox as well as a comforting truth. We know that in this life we will experience hours and perhaps days of grief and pain, but we also know that our heavenly Father is "the Father of mercies and the God of all comfort" (2 Cor. 1:3). Jesus the Son of God is "a man of sorrows and acquainted with grief" (Isa. 53:3) and is our interceding High Priest at the throne of grace (Heb. 4:14–16). The Holy Spirit is the Comforter who dwells in us and ministers to us (John 14:16, 20). We are comforted that we may be able to comfort others (2 Cor. 1:3–7). In the school of sorrow, God's people can learn many valuable lessons that cannot be learned any other way.

Let's meditate on three words in Paul's brief statement and see how this paradox points the way to Christian joy — no matter how painful our circumstances might be.

Sorrowful

Paul had more than his share of sorrows, the greatest of which was his "deep concern for all the churches" (2 Cor. 11:28). He wept over the people of Israel and prayed for their salvation (Rom. 10:1). He also wept over the worldly professed Christians in the churches (Phil. 3:17–21).

Having pastored three churches and counseled many pastors,

I can appreciate Paul's burden for God's people. Sorrow itself is not sinful unless it becomes so excessive that it paralyzes us or makes us do foolish things. I recall a distraught widower who wanted to pour a thick concrete slab over his wife's grave so the rain and snow could not reach the casket below. We may admire his love for his wife, but his sorrow was upsetting his common sense. Sorrow can make us selfish when it ought to make our hearts tender so that we seek to encourage others.

When Paul wrote his second letter to the Corinthian church, he was certainly experiencing sorrow. The church in Corinth was divided (1 Cor. 1:10–17), and some of the members were questioning Paul's apostolic authority. He was encouraging the Gentile churches to give generously to the offering he was receiving for the poor saints in Judea, but the church in Corinth was delaying their giving. Paul had to change his plans for visiting the Corinthian church and this had greatly upset some of the members. It seems that, no matter what God's servants do, there is always somebody in the church who misunderstands and starts criticizing and causing trouble.

In spite of what the health and wealth preachers tell us, Christians are not protected from suffering and sorrow. After all, the goal of the Christian life is likeness to Christ (Rom. 8:28–29), and He was a "man of sorrows and acquainted with grief" (Isa. 53:3). Paul experienced "the fellowship of His sufferings" (Phil. 3:10) even as he experienced the joy of the Lord. Instead of protecting us from battles and burdens, following Jesus Christ introduces us to problems and conflicts that occur only in the lives of believers. "In the world you will have tribulation," Jesus told His disciples, "but be of good cheer, I have overcome the world" (John 16:33).

Jesus compared our sorrows to the pains of a woman giving birth (John 16:20–22). This analogy tells us that our pain is not forever and that once it accomplishes its purposes, there will be joy. The same baby that causes the pain also causes the joy! "Weeping may endure for a night, but joy comes in the morning" (Ps. 30:5). In Gethsemane, Jesus faced the shame and agony of the cross and was overwhelmed by sorrow (Matt. 26:38); yet the Father heard His prayers and strengthened Him. Just as life brings us day and night and summer and winter, so it brings us pain and pleasure and joy and sorrow. All sunshine makes a desert, and all pleasure makes for immaturity and shallowness of character. Our loving Father balances for us the experiences of life so that we may mature and learn how to face difficulties courageously.

Because of the sin of our first parents, "the whole creation groans and labors with birth pangs together until now" (Rom. 8:22), and this situation definitely affects us. One night a tornado skipped over our house, pulled up a tall tree in the front yard, and threw it across the street. We were grateful it destroyed the tree and not our house. The body we live in and the world we inhabit are both part of a fallen creation that will not be delivered until Jesus returns to establish His kingdom. God is working out His divine plan and we are not able to explain all that He is doing, but we do know that He loves us and plans for us what is best. As the familiar song says, "I know not what the future holds, but I know Who holds the future."

Not only is fallen creation groaning, but our Savior groaned when He was ministering on earth. At the tomb of Lazarus, when Jesus saw His friends weeping, He "groaned in the spirit and was troubled" (John 11:33; see v. 38). He knew He was going to raise Lazarus from the dead, but that did not stop Him from entering into the pain of the two sisters and their friends. "Rejoice with those who rejoice, and weep with those who weep" (Rom. 12:15), and Jesus sets the example (Rom. 12:15).

When pain and sorrow come to people who do not know Christ, they usually turn to the world for help, which means distractions of one kind or another — alcohol, narcotics, entertainment, overeating, excessive shopping, and so on. What life does *to* us depends largely on what life finds *in* us, and if life is without faith in the Lord, it might fall apart. The unbeliever asks, "How can I get out of this?" but the child of God asks, "What can I get out of this?" The steady faith of the Christian in days of difficulty is a great testimony to the unbelieving world. Times of difficulty can also be times of discovery, not only of our own needs but also of God's gracious supply. The Holy Spirit helps us in our praying "and makes intercession for us with groanings which cannot be uttered" (Rom. 8:26). In that same chapter (v. 23), Paul tells us that each believer groans within, longing for the new glorified body that we will have when we see Jesus.

Rejoicing

We have so many reasons to rejoice, even when the days are dark and the nights are long and lonely. God is our Father, Jesus is our Savior and our interceding High Priest, and the Holy Spirit is our Comforter. What more do we need? The Bible nourishes us, guides us, and supports our faith with promise after promise. God's throne is a throne of grace, not of judgment. Our Christian friends love us, pray for us, and encourage us. The adequate grace that we receive from the Lord we can share with others who are hurting, even as they share with us. We become channels of blessing when we think we have been drained of every bit of strength.

Happiness depends primarily on happenings, but joy in the Lord goes far deeper. It is not based on what *we* are doing but on what the Lord has already done for us. "The eternal God is your refuge, and underneath are the everlasting arms" (Deut. 33:27). "Do not sorrow, for the joy of the LORD is your strength" (Neh. 8:10). Joy is not something we manufacture ourselves; it is one of the fruits of the Spirit that we cultivate as we walk in the Spirit and are led by the Spirit (Gal. 5:16–18, 22–23). No matter what sorrows invade our lives, we can be joyful in the Lord. This does not mean that we bury our sorrows and pretend they do not exist, for that approach only makes things worse. When we talk to the Lord, we tell Him how we feel, and we acknowledge that we need His grace and wisdom. We thank Him for the blessings He sends that give us joy, and we trust Him to do it again — and again.

"I now rejoice in my sufferings for you," Paul wrote to the Colossian believers when he was a Roman prisoner (Col. 2:24); and to the church in Philippi, he wrote, "Yes, and if I am being poured out as a drink offering on the sacrifice and service of your faith, I am glad and rejoice with you all. For the same reason you also be glad and rejoice with me" (Phil. 2:17–18). His correspondence was saturated with joy! Paul realized that his situation in prison opened doors of opportunity that he might not otherwise have, and the blessing God was giving would benefit the churches who were praying for him. In times of sorrow and pain, we must not focus only on ourselves but also on others. Like Jesus on the cross, we must pray for others, encourage others, and care for others. When times are difficult, anyone can spread sorrow; but it takes a Spirit-filled Christian to share the joy of the Lord when it would be easy to complain and get sympathy.

But our joy must be "in the Lord" and not be an act we put on to fool people. If it comes from the heart, it is real; if it comes only from the lips, it is phony. If we turn our joy on and off like a light switch, we are only hurting ourselves. The familiar children's song that says "Jesus and others and you/what a wonderful way to spell joy" says it perfectly. I can recall making hospital visits on people whose joyful courage sent me away singing the doxology. I wanted to be a blessing to them and they beat me to it!

Always

According to the communications experts, "always" and "never" are two words we need to keep under careful control. Only the Lord knows what people always or never do and say. The coach who says to the student "You always strike out" or the parent who tells a child "You always leave your room in a mess" will not solve the problem. Neither will the husband who says to his wife, "You never remember to buy toothpaste." If these people are keeping records of what others are doing wrong, they are not very good Christians. First Corinthians 13:6 tells us that "love keeps no record of wrongs" (NIV). If we use "always" and "never" for the good things, we will accomplish more. "You always remember to buy gas" and "Son, you never forget to wash the car" create a healthy atmosphere of positive love and action.

But Paul was an inspired apostle who often used "always" in his letters. In 2 Corinthians he uses "always" six times, so let's study these verses in three categories and discover what "always" has to do with rejoicing and sorrowing.

We begin with 2 Corinthians 2:14, "Now thanks be to God who always leads us in triumph in Christ, and through us diffuses the fragrance of His knowledge in every place." The picture here is that of the "Roman triumph" parade that honored a commander-in-chief whose army had won complete victory over the enemy on foreign soil and had slain at least five thousand enemy soldiers. The commander gained new territory for Rome and brought home not only captives but valuable spoils. Paul sees in this parade a picture of what Jesus Christ accomplished in His death, burial, and resurrection; for Calvary was a complete victory over the devil (Col. 2:15). Jesus is always triumphant (2 Cor. 2:12–17) and we are triumphant through Him; but we must follow Him and obey orders, for He "*leads* us in triumph."

Second Corinthians 4:9–12 gives us Paul's second use of "always": "persecuted, but not forsaken; struck down, but not destroyed — always carrying about in the body the dying of the Lord Jesus, that the life of Jesus also may be manifested in our body. For we who live are always delivered to death for Jesus' sake, that the life of Jesus also may be manifested in our mortal flesh. So then death is working in us, but life in you." If we know that Christ died for us, we can trust Him and be saved. But if we also know that *we died with Christ*, we can have victory over the old sinful nature that wants to drag us down. Paul's testimony was, "I have been crucified with Christ" (Gal. 2:20). He deals with this great truth in Romans 6, a chapter every believer should master. We died with Christ so that we can overcome the old nature, and we arose to walk with Christ so we can serve Him in victory. Paul led a life filled with danger and wrote "in deaths often" (2 Cor. 11:23), but he had died to the old life and thought only of living for Christ regardless of the dangers involved. Jesus explained this in John 12:20–26, so pause and take time to read the passage.

Second Corinthians 5:1–8 picks up the theme of the death of the Christian's body and Paul uses the phrase "we are always confident" (v. 6). Confident of what? Confident of being with Jesus in heaven if and when we die! Confident of having a new glorified body! The English word "confident" comes from the Latin *con* ("with") and *fide* ("faith"). "For we walk by faith, not by sight" (v. 7). We thank God for those courageous men and women who blazed the missionary trails, willing to lay down their lives for the sake of the gospel. "For to me, to live is Christ, and to die is gain" (Phil. 1:21). No matter where the Lord sends us, we can be confident of His care.

We have already considered "always rejoicing" (2 Cor. 6:10), so all that remains is 9:8: "And God is able to make all grace abound toward you, that you, always having all sufficiency in all things, have an abundance for every good work." What a statement! It beats any guarantee that the wealthiest and most powerful person in the world could make. We have all grace, not carefully measured out but abounding. We always have all sufficiency in all things, and we can draw upon all the abundance we need for every good work God calls us to do. All grace! Always! All sufficiency! All things! Every good work! We need not worry about life or death, poverty or pain, loss of resources, or having to face any challenge the Lord presents. All of the alls belong to us! "And my God shall supply all your needs according to His riches in glory by Christ Jesus" (Phil. 4:19).

One of the best definitions of peace I have ever read is, "Peace is the possession of adequate resources." There is no reason why God's people should worry when their Father in heaven has given them such incredible promises. And the promise of Philippians 4:19 measures the supply "according to His riches in glory." Not "out of His riches," for then the supply might dwindle; but it is "according to His riches." The supply will never be used up! Paul's Ephesians letter is our "bankbook" with its emphasis on the riches we share in Jesus Christ: the riches of His grace (1:7–8; 2:7); the riches of His glory (1:18; 3:16); and the unsearchable [boundless, fathomless, exhaustless] riches of Christ (3:8).

Yes, there are sorrows that come our way, but by the boundless grace of God, we may be always rejoicing in the midst of sorrows to the glory of God! This leads us to one more "always" verse (though it is outside of 2 Cor.): "giving thanks always for all things to God the Father in the name of our Lord Jesus Christ" (Eph. 5:20). Always thankful!

Are we?

We should be!

11

We Lead Others by Serving Them

O LORD, I pray, please let Your ear be attentive to the prayer of Your servant, and to the prayer of Your servants who desire to fear Your name; and let Your servant prosper this day, I pray, and grant him mercy in the sight of this man." For I was the king's cupbearer. (Neh. 1:11)

His lord said to him, "Well done, good and faithful servant; you have been faithful over a few things, I will make you ruler over many things. Enter into the joy of your lord." (Matt. 25:21)

The kings of the Gentiles exercise lordship over them, and those who exercise authority over them are called "benefactors." But not so among you; on the contrary, he who is greatest among you, let him be as the younger, and he who governs as he who serves. For who is greater, he who sits at the table, or he who serves? Is it not he who sits at the table? Yet I am among you as the One who serves. (Luke 22:25–27)

If anyone serves Me, let him follow Me; and where I am, there My servant will be also. If anyone serves Me, him will My Father honor. (John 12:26).

But now having been set free from sin, and having become slaves of God, you have your fruit to holiness, and the end, everlasting life. (Rom. 6:22)

Let a man so consider us, as servants of Christ and stewards of the mysteries of God. (1 Cor. 4:1)

For even when we were with you, we commanded you this: If anyone will not work, neither will he eat. (2 Thess. 3:10)

For this is the will of God, that by doing good you may put to silence the ignorance of sinful men — as free, yet not losing your liberty as a cloak for vice, but as bondservants of God. (1 Peter 2:15–16)

FOR THE MOST PART, the Greeks and Romans in New Testament times despised manual labor. Many of them turned their work over to their slaves and simply gave orders. The ancients dreamed of a paradise where nobody had to work hard.

The Jewish population, however, had a work ethic that came down from heaven: "Six days shall you labor and do all your work, but the seventh day is the Sabbath of the Lord your God. In it you shall do no work" (Exod. 20:9–10). It was as important for the Jewish people to work on the six days as it was to rest on the seventh day. For them, work was a normal part of life.

Our Lord Jesus carried this work ethic a step further and taught His disciples that the best way to be a leader was to be a servant and work, and He set the example. "I am among you as the One who serves" (Luke 22:27).

Our Lord's paradox that we lead by serving is desperately needed today. I fear we have many so-called leaders who only serve themselves and ignore the workers to whom they should be ministering. There are organizations (including churches) with

leaders who are obviously dictators and attract people who find
security in being controlled by strong leaders, instead of being
matured by a caring shepherd who equips them to grow and serve.
Needless to say, these so-called leaders are not leading and their
followers are not maturing.

In order for us to imitate our Savior as leaders who serve, we
must understand three fundamental facts.

We Live in a Working World

God created it that way. From the mineral kingdom through the
vegetable, animal, and human kingdoms, each level of creation
makes its contribution to the others. The vegetable kingdom
reaches down into the mineral kingdom for sustenance, and the
animal kingdom sustains life partly from the vegetable kingdom.
The human kingdom reaches down to the vegetable and animal
kingdoms where the Lord has placed just what we need for maintaining a healthy life. Trees and flowers and brooks and humming-
birds and cows and rays of sunshine are all working for us day and
night whether we realize it or not. Whenever this essential cycle
of mutual subsistence is broken, the human family suffers. Most
people take this miracle natural cycle for granted day after day, but
Christian believers joyfully sing "This is my Father's world" and
give Him thanks for His wisdom and generosity.

We must not make the mistake of thinking that employment
is punishment and that we must labor because our first parents
sinned. *Adam worked in the Garden of Eden before sin entered the
human race* (Gen. 2:15). It was not until the man and the woman
disobeyed God that work became toil (Gen. 3:17–19). The Lord
wanted mankind to live in a beautiful and fruitful garden, but sin
changed all of that. And we will not be in God's garden until we
see Jesus (Rev. 21–22). Meanwhile, each of us has divinely assigned

work to do and we must faithfully do it. "Whatever your hands find to do, do it with your might" (Eccl. 9:10). Ecclesiastes 5:19 tells us our work is a gift from God, and that we should rejoice in the privilege of working. We may change vocations several times on our journey of life; but if we are in the will of God, we will find satisfaction in what the Lord assigns us to do. According to Jesus, doing the Father's will is nourishment, not punishment (John 4:31–34); and if we do His will from the heart, it will pay rich dividends in many ways, besides giving us a salary.

When God created the world, the angels praised Him and shouted for joy (Job 38:4–7), and we ought to join them, in spite of what the human race has done to exploit and destroy God's creation. Even when we reach the time of retirement when regular work is no longer a part of life, the Lord still has service plans for us. When a team of doctors told me and my wife it was time to stop traveling in ministry, we wondered what our next assignment would be. It did not take long to find out, for lay church leaders and busy pastors began to ask for counsel and times of instruction, and this mentoring ministry has been most delightful. I'm still writing (or you would not have this book) and my wife and I are doing what we can to encourage God's people and help build God's church.

I have counted twenty-six verses in the book of Proverbs that deal with laziness (the sluggard) and whose promises and warnings are applicable today. From early childhood, I was taught to do my share of the work at home; and when I was old enough, I earned money doing odd jobs in our neighborhood, mowing lawns, washing windows, and such. I may not have earned a great deal of money, but the discipline and exercise did me good and my parents never had to give me an allowance. I tell people that it's a good thing I'm retired or I could not handle all the work I have to do!

We Follow a Serving Savior

Many people found in the Scriptures are called "servants of God," including Abraham (Ps. 105:42), Moses (Num. 12:7), Caleb (Num. 14:24), Job (42:7–8), Isaiah (20:3), Nebuchadnezzar (Jer. 25:9), and the apostle Paul (Rom. 1:1). But the greatest servant of all in the Bible is Jesus Christ, the Son of God (Isa. 42:1–7; Phil. 2:5–8). What a price He paid to lay aside His heavenly glory and come to earth as a servant! He grew up in a working man's home and was called "the carpenter" (Mark 6:3). Being fully human, Jesus knew what it meant to be weary, hungry, and thirsty. Once He was so weary that He fell asleep in the boat in the midst of a great storm that frightened His fishermen disciples (Matt. 8:23–24).

It was demanding for our Lord to minister to the crowds who followed Him from place to place day after day, in the synagogues and in the temple. He preached the good news of salvation, taught the principles of the kingdom of God, healed the sick and afflicted, commanded the demons to depart, and even raised the dead. People pressed Him in the crowds that they might touch the hem of His garment and be delivered. Day after day, His enemies watched Him carefully, plotting against Him and wanting to kill Him. He sometimes prayed all night, and day after day arose early in the morning to meet with the Father in prayer (Mark 1:35; see Isa. 50:4–6). I have had my busy days of ministry, but the faithful ministry of Jesus on earth is beyond anything I can imagine.

"My Father has been working until now," said Jesus, "and I have been working" (John 5:17). He also said, "I must work the works of Him who sent Me while it is day; the night is coming when no one can work" (John 9:4). "The Father has not left Me alone, for I always do those things that please Him" (John 8:29). "My food is to do the will of Him who sent Me, and to finish His work" (John 4:34). "For I have come down from heaven, not to do My own will, but the will of Him who sent Me" (John 6:38). In His prayer before His arrest, Jesus told His Father, "I have glorified You on the earth. I have finished the work which You have given Me to do" (John 17:4). May all of us be able to say those words when our earthly walk comes to an end!

In obedience to the Father and out of love beyond measure, our Lord willingly gave His life on the cross that sinners might be forgiven and have an eternal home in heaven. The Roman soldiers nailed some boards to make a cross and then nailed the Carpenter from heaven on that cross to die for you and me. The greatest Worker who ever lived on this earth finished the greatest work ever done on this earth. If Jesus is my Savior and Lord, then I must follow His example and finish the work He has called me to do.

During these more than seventy years of knowing the Lord and seeking to serve Him, it has been a special blessing to work together with other believers — people Paul called "God's fellow workers" (1 Cor. 3:9). I am so grateful that we do not labor alone, sacrifice alone, suffer alone, or obey Jesus alone. We are "all one in Christ Jesus" (Gal. 3:28), laboring together to reach the lost and encourage the saved. What an encouragement it is to know that "it is God who works in you both to will and to do for His good pleasure" (Phil. 2:13). We follow a serving Savior and rejoice that we are servants of the Most High God!

Jesus humbled Himself to come to earth to be a servant, and His disciples needed to learn the meaning of humility — as do all of us. One day He asked the twelve what they had been arguing about as they walked on the way, and they had to admit they were debating over which of them was the greatest. They were promoting competition, not cooperation; and imitating the world, not their Master. Jesus put a child in their midst and told them to be childlike, which suggests submission, obedience, gratitude, faith, and dependence (Matt. 18:1–5). Jesus said, "But he who is greatest among you shall be your servant" (Matt. 23:11). Jesus serves us today as our Advocate (1 John 2:1) and our High Priest (Heb. 4:14–16), and He has promised, "I am with you always, even to the end of the age" (Matt. 28:20).

We Believe a Faithful Formula

Life is serious for everybody but especially for Christians. To begin with, life is short and gives us the only opportunity we will ever have to prepare for eternity. When we come to the end of our journey and stand before our Savior at the judgment seat of Christ, if we have ignored God's will and messed up our lives, our reward will be minimal, if at all. Life is serious because life is a stewardship from God, and "it is required in stewards that one be found faithful" (1 Cor. 4:2). The Lord does not command us to be "successful" as the world measures success, but He does command us to be faithful and do His will — come what may. If we have been faithful to obey, our Savior will be faithful to reward. If we have foolishly wasted our opportunities, we will receive no reward. "For we shall all stand before the judgment seat of Christ" (Rom. 14:10).

Twice in the parable of the talents (Matt. 25:14–30), our Lord gives us the formula for true success in life. "Well done, good and faithful servant; you were faithful over a few things, I will make you ruler over many things. Enter into the joy of your Lord" (Matt. 25:21, 23). I will explain this formula in detail later, but first I must define some words.

Today we use the word "talents" to mean the natural abilities people were born with, but the parable tells us that the master of the house gave the servants talents *according to their abilities*. Those talents were pieces of money, and they represented opportunities to use their abilities in serving their master (Matt. 25:15). Our Master gave us our abilities when we were born, and our spiritual gifts when we were born again, and He wants us to use those gifts and abilities for His glory. My two older brothers had remarkable mechanical and athletic abilities, but I did not. So the Lord has never called me to manage a football team or repair an automobile. If He did, He would have to give me the know-how I needed to be successful.

The success principle illustrated in the parable is this: if we are faithful to the Lord in using our abilities and gifts as He provides opportunities (the talents), then we will go from servants to rulers, from few things to many things, and from toil to joy (vv. 21, 23). The man in the parable who buried his one talent gave up his opportunity to please his master and get a reward. God wants us to invest what He gives us and not simply protect it; and we should be ready to report to the Savior when we stand at His judgment seat.

We begin as servants and, if we are faithful, we become leaders. You find this pattern illustrated throughout Scripture. Joseph was hated by his brothers, sold as a slave, and taken to Egypt. He was such a good worker that his master put him in charge of his whole household, but his master's wife lied about Joseph and he was put in jail. But even there Joseph was faithful in helping the jail keeper and the other prisoners. His wisdom came to the attention of pharaoh who was troubled because he did not know the meaning of his two dreams. Joseph explained the dreams and pharaoh made him the second ruler in Egypt. Joseph went from few things to many things, from servant to ruler, and from toil to joy.

Moses had a similar experience as he moved from being a shepherd to becoming a prophet and the leader of the people of Israel. Joshua was Moses' personal aide and he became Moses' successor and the conqueror of the Promised Land. David also began as a shepherd and became king of Israel. Ruth went to Bethlehem a destitute widow but was faithful and became the wife of a wealthy citizen and the ancestress of the house of David. Her name is in our Lord's genealogy (Matt. 1:5–6). The supreme example is our Lord Jesus Christ who was faithful in His ministry, suffered, sacrificed, and died but arose again and is now King of kings and Lord of lords (Rev. 17:14; 19:16; Phil. 2:5–11).

We lead by serving. If we want to go from servants to rulers, from few things to many things, and from toil to joy, we must live by faith and practice humility, obedience, and patience.

Over the years, I have faithfully read my Bible as well as hundreds of biographies and autobiographies, and I can assure you that there are no easy roads or cheap shortcuts to the kind of success that honors the Lord and helps to change the world. If you think that there are, just recall the story Jesus told about the prodigal son (Luke 15:11–32). This young man made a mess out of his life by ignoring obedience, humility, and patience. He started with many things and ended up with nothing. He started with worldly pleasure and ended up with toil. And he started with being important with all his wealth and ended up a disappointed slave, bankrupt and feeding the pigs. You can hardly call that success.

Revelation 22:3 grips my attention because it describes the eternal future of God's people: "And there shall be no more curse, but the throne of God and of the Lamb shall be in it [the new Jerusalem], and His servants shall serve Him." Yes, there will be rest and praise in our heavenly home, but there will also be service to render to our Lord. The service we render in eternity will depend on the kind of service we rendered during our lifetime here on earth. Scripture does not go into detail, but it does make it clear that how we serve today determines the ministry the Lord will give us in the new heaven and the new earth (Matt. 24:45–51; 25:14–30). It is not easy to determine the details, but the fact is there that the Lord has ministries prepared in the new heaven and the new earth for all His faithful servants.

The Greek word translated "serve" in Revelation 22:3 is a word used for the worship of God (*latreuō*). At the entrance of many church sanctuaries there is often a sign that reads ENTER TO WORSHIP, and when you leave the sanctuary, you see a sign that says DEPART TO SERVE. But in heaven, service and worship will be united: our service will be worship and our worship will be service. I confess that there have been times in the past seventy plus years when my worship on earth has been difficult and my service for the Lord has been a burden, but it will never be that way in heaven. Every thought, word, and deed will always be worship and service to the glory of the Lord.

We live in a working world. Do we work as diligently in serving the Lord as we do performing our daily tasks? We follow a serving Savior. Do we imitate Jesus Christ so that the Father can say to us, "Well done, good and faithful servant"? The Lord has given us a faithful formula for success in the Christian life. Are we obeying it or imitating the ways of the world?

We lead others by serving others.

There is no other way.

12

Knowing Love That Passes Knowledge

> *For this reason I bow my knees to the Father of our Lord Jesus Christ, from whom the whole family in heaven and earth is named, that He would grant you, according the riches of His glory, to be strengthened with might through through His Spirit in the inner man, that Christ may dwell in your hearts through faith; that you, being rooted and grounded in love, may be able to comprehend with all the saints what is the width and length and depth and height — to know the love of Christ that passes knowledge; that you may be filled with all the fullness of God. Now to Him who is able to do exceedingly abundantly above all that we ask or think, according to the power that works in us, to Him be glory in the church by Christ Jesus to all generation, forever and ever. Amen. (Eph. 3:14–21)*

IT IS POSSIBLE FOR YOU AND ME to operate equipment we do not understand and also to have experiences we cannot explain. I do not understand how my computer functions, but in my own clumsy way I can compose letters on it and even write books. I know how to drive my automobile, but when it is not working properly, I do not know what is wrong or how to make things right. I am at the mercy of the technicians and I thank God for them.

But a similar phenomenon shows up in the normal Christian life: *we can experience but we cannot always explain.* The apostle Paul assures us we can even "know the love of Christ that passes knowledge" (Eph. 3:19)! What a paradox: knowing the unknowable!

Paul's prayer in Ephesians 3:14–21 emphasizes the importance of God's love in our prayer life. Usually in Scripture, prayer is associated with faith, but this text relates prayer to love. The vast dimensions of the love of Christ should touch every aspect of the Christian life, from the meals we eat to the work we do, the thoughts we think, and the plans we make. We should grow in our spiritual understanding of the love of Christ and His intercession for us, even though that love is beyond mere human comprehension. Accepting this "love paradox" of Christian prayer can help us grow in both our love for Jesus and our ministry of prayer.

What are we actually doing when we pray, not only in faith but also in the power of the love of Jesus Christ? Paul's prayer gives us the answers.

We Are Sharing in Building the Church

Paul opened his prayer with a significant phrase: "For this reason" (v. 14). For what reason? For the reason mentioned in verses *Eph. 2* 19–22 — the building of the church of Jesus Christ on this earth. Before He began His public ministry, Jesus worked as a carpenter in Joseph's shop in Nazareth (Matt. 13:55; Mark 6:3). Since His ascension to heaven, Jesus has been building a home in heaven for His people (John 14:1–6) as well as His church here on earth (Matt. 16:13–20). I have heard pastors say, "Well, at my church..." and I want to remind them that Jesus is building *His* church, not ours. But we can do our part by the use of our witness, our prayers, our ministry, and our gifts.

Besides picturing the church as a building, Paul also uses the images of the family (3:15), the human body (4:16), and the army (6:10–20) to illustrate the significance of the church. Note that Paul also uses the word "whole": the whole family, the whole building, and the whole body. The church and its spiritual gifts are not for a "special elite" but for all who have trusted Jesus as their Savior and Lord. Satan hates the church and does all he can to hinder its ministries and attack its people. One of Satan's names is "destroyer" (called "Abaddon" and "Apollyon" in Rev. 9:11); and from his deception of Eve (Gen. 3) to his final judgment, he opposes the work of the church. When our prayers are motivated by love, we are helping to build and strengthen Christ's church.

We Are Submitting to the Will of God (3:14)

In his praying, Paul bowed his knees in submission to the Father. It has well been said that the purpose of prayer is not to get man's will done in heaven but to get God's will done on earth (1 John 5:14–15). There is no neutral ground: we either submit or rebel. A number of postures are mentioned in the Ephesians epistle: being raised from the dead and seated with Christ (2:1–6), bowing in prayer (3:14), walking in obedience (4:1), and standing alert as a soldier and ready for battle (6:10–20). If we are seated with Christ, we share His power and authority and "reign in life" (Rom. 5:17). Paul's prayer in Ephesians 3:14–21 emphasizes the strength and power the Lord shares with us as we "trust and obey." Remember, we are fighting *from* Christ's victory over Satan and not *for* victory in our own strength. In His death, resurrection, ascension to glory, and enthronement in heaven, Christ declares total victory and shares it with us. Praise God, for in Him we are overcomers!

We Are Encouraging God's People (v. 15)

We are part of "the whole family of God," and our Father wants us to pray not only for ourselves and our needs but also for others in the family. I am encouraged when people tell me they are praying for me. I have received letters from strangers assuring me of their prayer support and I write and thank them and pray for them. We certainly ought to pray for the lost because "the Lord desires all men to be saved" (1 Tim. 2:4) and is "not willing that any should perish but that all should come to repentance" (2 Peter 3:9). "Some people think that God does not want to be troubled with our constant coming and asking," said evangelist D. L. Moody. "The only way to trouble God is *not to come at all!*" Charles Haddon Spurgeon told his ministerial students, "However, brethren, whether we like it or not, asking is the rule of the kingdom." Why are we lacking what we need? "You do not have because you do not ask" (James 4:2). Frederick Beck wrote, "If you are swept off your feet, it is time to get on your knees."

Keep in mind that that our heavenly High Priest is constantly interceding for us (Heb. 7:25; Rom. 8:34) and so is the indwelling Holy Spirit (Rom. 8:26–27). Is there any reason why we should not be interceding for others? Prayer should be motivated by love as well as by faith. "Prayer is the most important thing in my life," said Martin Luther. "If I should neglect prayer for a single day, I should lose a great deal of the fire of faith."

We Are Maturing in Our Christian Life (vv. 16–17)

These verses describe the changes that take place in the life of the Christian who has a consistent prayer life that is bathed in love. We have available from the riches of the Father's grace all the wisdom and enablement we need to do His will and glorify

His name. We may feel unable to serve our Lord, but He will turn our weakness into strength as He did for Paul (2 Cor. 12:7–10).

Prayer not only transforms us from weakness to strength and power, but it also transforms us from shallowness to depth (Eph. 4:17). Shallow worship and shallow preaching produce shallow Christians. How tragic it is when we live on "baby food" and ignore the solid food that is the diet of maturing Christians (Heb. 6). In view of the way believers are being persecuted in different parts of the world today, our churches need mature spiritual leadership and depth of worship as never before. Our world is a battleground and not a playground. "Watch, stand fast in the faith, be brave, be strong" (1 Cor. 16:13).

Paul uses three words that speak of depth: "dwell," "rooted," and "grounded." The word translated "dwell" means "to settle down and feel at home." By His Spirit, our Lord dwells within our hearts, and the way we treat the Spirit is the way we treat the Savior. Someone has said that Jesus should be president and not just resident, and this is true. Jesus cannot feel at home in our hearts if we grieve the Spirit, lie to the Spirit, or resist the Spirit. If we are to enjoy the blessings of the Spirit of God, we must make sure He feels at home. This means we must have a clean heart, an obedient will, a mind filled with God's truth, and a deep desire to glorify the Lord in all that we say and do.

If the Savior does not feel at home in my heart, He cannot bless my life or my ministry and He cannot answer my prayers. "If I regard iniquity in my heart, the Lord will not hear" (Ps. 66:18). In Genesis 18 and 19, our Lord visited Abraham personally, but He sent two angels to visit Lot who was living in wicked Sodom. Our Lord did not feel at home in Lot's house, but He felt very much at home with Abraham and blessed him. Jesus felt at home with Mary, Martha, and Lazarus in Bethany (Luke 10:38–42; John 12:1–8) but He was unhappy in the home of Simon the Pharisee whose heart was not right (Luke 7:36–49). Does He feel at home in our hearts, homes, and church fellowships? (Matt. 18:20).

The second depth word in Ephesians 3:17 is "rooted," which speaks of vegetation. The believer God blesses is rooted by the river, for in Scripture, water for drinking is a picture of the Holy Spirit (John 7:37–39; Ps. 1:1–3). We must be "rooted and built up in Him and established in the faith" (Col. 2:7). Sad to say, many professed believers are more like tumbleweeds than like trees, for they "are tossed to and fro and carried about with every wind of doctrine" (Eph. 4:14). The roots stabilize the tree and keep it steadfast when the storms threaten. Without the nourishment brought by the roots, the tree cannot produce fruit and be a blessing to people.

Not only should we be rooted but we should also be "grounded," which is an architectural term that means "established on a good foundation." It reminds us of our Lord's parable about the two builders (Matt. 7:24–29). If we do not build our lives on obedience to the word of God, we are building on the sand, and what we build will not last. It takes time and disciplined hard work to lay the foundation, but without a strong foundation, the structure will not stand.

Two of the congregations my wife and I served had to go through building programs. In the first church, the old building was demolished and we built a new sanctuary. In the second, we built a new and larger sanctuary adjacent to the old building, and it seemed like the workmen were digging the foundation forever. Day after day, I looked into that deep hole; and finally I asked the architect, "When will we get out of this hole?" His reply was one of the best one-sentence sermons I have ever heard: "Preacher, if you don't go down deep, you can't go up high." Problem settled.

We Are Expanding Our Spiritual Capacity (vv. 18–19)

As children grow up, the body gets larger, and so does the world they live in, including their vocabularies, responsibilities, and opportunities. And so should it be with every child of God. As we read and study the Bible, fellowship with the church family in worship and prayer, learn from faithful pastors and teachers, and serve the Lord as He opens doors for us, we should grow in every area of the Christian life. Even though we cannot measure the vastness of the dimensions of God's love, we can receive from Him the daily measure that we are able to hold and appreciate. Enjoyment of His love brings about enlargement in His love; and as we grow in grace and knowledge, we grow in spiritual capacity.

What is the width of God's world? "For God so loved the world" (John 3:16). What is the length of His love? A cross where God "spared not His own Son" (Rom. 8:32). What is the depth of His love? Jesus Christ was made sin for us (2 Cor. 5:21). What is the height of His love? "I go to prepare a place for you" (John 14:1–6). The more we ponder these dimensions, the more we grow in our love for Christ and our understanding of God's grace, and the greater becomes our capacity for loving God and one another — and a lost world.

We Are Bringing Glory to God

God's strength and fullness are available to us if we sincerely seek to glorify Him and not ourselves. Note that each member of the Godhead is mentioned in this prayer in Ephesians 3: Father (vv. 14–16) and Son (vv. 17, 19, 21) and Holy Spirit (v. 16). The Son glorifies the Father (John 13:31–32) and the Spirit glorifies the Son (John 16:13–15).

Note that the Spirit desires to glorify Jesus by working through each individual believer: "the power that works in us" (Eph. 3:20). It is not enough just to pray; we must also be available to the Lord *for Him to use us to answer prayer*. It is foolish to give the Lord requests and then become spectators and not participants. We must imitate Isaiah the prophet and say, "Here am I! Send me" (Isa. 6:8). Moses longed for the Lord to deliver the people of Israel from Egypt, and the Lord sent *him* to do the job. Nehemiah wept because of the ruins of Jerusalem and prayed for God to act, and God called *him* to supervise the work. Gideon was burdened because the Midianites had invaded Israel, and God appointed *him* to lead the army to victory. While worshiping in church one Lord's day, Hudson Taylor felt a great burden for China and left the joyful service and went for a walk, praying for the Chinese and giving himself wholly to the Lord. God's call came to *him,* and the next day he opened a bank account in the name of the China Inland Mission. "Here am I! Send me."

I heard about a father who was leading his wife and children in family prayer and especially praying for the missionaries. When he had finished praying, one of the children said, "Daddy, if I had your checkbook, I could answer your prayers." That child understood "the power that works in us." We cannot do everything, but we can do something, and God will provide the power. We are exhorted in Jude 21, "Keep yourselves in the love of God," and it is obedience to the Lord that does this. "If you love Me," said Jesus, "keep My commandments" (John 14:15). "God does not want our success," said Chuck Colson, "He wants us. He does not demand our achievements; He demands our obedience." John R. W. Stott said, "Greatness in the kingdom of God is measured in terms of obedience."

We can never calculate the dimensions of the love of God nor can we fully know "the love of Christ that passes knowledge" (Eph. 3:19). But these "dimension statements" from Scripture assure us that there is plenty of love for everybody forever! In Romans 8:35–39, Paul makes it clear that nothing can separate us from God's love, but Jude 21 warns us that God's children can separate themselves from God's love — and that is exactly what the church at Ephesus did! Jesus said to them, "Nevertheless I have this against you, that you have left your first love" (Rev. 2:4; see 2:1–7). There was much about the church at Ephesus that Jesus could commend, but their ministry was not motivated by love for Jesus Christ. We can be busy reading the Scriptures, praying, helping others, serving at church, and even making sacrifices, but if what we do does not flow from a heart of love for Christ, the Lord cannot accept it (see 1 Cor. 13:1–3). The godly missionary Amy Carmichael reminds us, "You can give without loving, but you cannot love without giving."

God wants both.

paradox

13

We See the Invisible

In the beginning God created the heavens and the earth. The earth was without form, and void; and darkness was on the face of the deep. And the Spirit of God was hovering over the face of the waters. Then God said, "Let there be light"; and there was light. And God saw the light, that it was good; and God divided the light from the darkness. (Gen. 1:1–4)

And when the servant of the man of God arose early and went out, there was an army, surrounding the city with horses and chariots. And his servant said to him, "Alas, my master! What shall we do?" So he answered. "Do not fear, for those who are with us are more than those who are with them." And Elisha prayed, and said, "LORD, I pray, open his eyes that he may see." Then the LORD opened the eyes of the young man, and he saw. And behold, the mountain was full of horses and chariots of fire all around Elisha. (2 Kings 6:15–17)

Open my eyes, that I may see wondrous things from Your Law. (Ps. 119:18)

Your word is a lamp to my feet and a light to my path. (Ps. 119:105)

Jesus answered and said to [Nicodemus], "Most assuredly, I say to you, except one is born again, he cannot see the kingdom of God. . . . And this is the condemnation, that the light has come into the world, and men loved darkness rather than light, because their deeds were evil. For everyone practicing evil hates the light and does not come to the light, lest his deeds should be exposed. But he who does the truth comes to the light, that his deeds may be clearly seen, that they have been done in God." (John 3:3, 19–21)

By faith [Moses] forsook Egypt, not fearing the wrath of the king; for he endured as seeing Him who is invisible. (Heb. 11:27)

And the city had no need of the sun or of the moon to shine in it, for the glory of God illuminated it, and the Lamb is its light. (Rev. 21:23)

WE HAVE REMARKABLE scientific instruments today that enable us to penetrate the microscopic world, contemplate outer space and the world of nature around us, and investigate the human body with its many cells and organs and afflictions. I am personally grateful for my kit that helps me measure my blood sugar, and I appreciate my ophthalmologist who checks my eyes each month and does what is necessary to keep me from going blind. (My almanac tells me that each year 12,000 to 24,000 diabetics may lose their eyesight, and I do not want to be a part of that statistic.) I also have an audiologist who services my hearing aids. Believe me, getting old has its problems! In my case, my eyes get the most attention, and I thank the Lord for the people and the equipment that make this possible.

The Lord created us to see and we must never take this privilege for granted. I am writing this chapter on a lovely spring day, and after dinner, I plan to sit with my wife on the patio and admire the flowers in the garden, observe the birds and squirrels coming and going, and watch the shades of evening creep in. As long as it is light, I will probably read a book. Without eyesight, all of this would be impossible.

But there is another kind of sight that is very important and also must be cultivated and protected, and that is the kind of spiritual sight that Moses had, for he could see the invisible (Heb. 11:27). I remember hearing Vance Havner say in a sermon that "Moses saw the invisible, chose the imperishable, and did the impossible" (see Heb. 11:23–29). But this privilege does not belong only to great leaders like Moses, for the Lord offers it to all of His children. As Jesus told Nicodemus, when you are born again, your spiritual eyes are opened to behold the wonders of the kingdom of God (John 3:3). And as you grow spiritually, you see the invisible and rejoice in the beauty and bounty of that kingdom. There are four stages in this experience as we move from blindness to sight, from sight to insight, from insight to vision, and from vision to reality.

Blindness: The Unsaved Cannot See the Things of God

When Jesus came to earth, people were sitting in spiritual darkness and unable to find the light (Matt. 4:13–16; Isa. 9:1–2). The Lord sent John the Baptist to prepare them to receive the glorious life-changing light that Jesus is and gives (John 8:12). "There was a man sent from God, whose name was John. This man came for a witness, to bear witness of the Light, that all through him might believe. He was not that Light, but was sent to bear witness of that Light. That was the true Light which gives light to every man who comes into the world" (John 1:6–9).

The only people who must be told that the light is shining are blind people, and our world today is spiritually blind!

As you read through John's Gospel, you meet spiritually blind people who did not understand what Jesus was teaching. In chapter 2, the crowd thought He was talking about their temple (vv. 13–22). In chapter 3, Nicodemus thought our Lord was speaking about physical birth (vv. 1–4). In chapter 4, the Samaritan woman thought of physical water, not spiritual water (vv. 1–15). The Jewish crowd in chapter 6 had no understanding of spiritual bread come down from heaven or what it meant to eat His flesh and drink His blood (vv. 22–58). When He spoke of spiritual freedom, the Jews thought of political freedom (8:31–36). I could go on, but I am sure you get the point. If lost sinners are truly seeking salvation, the Holy Spirit will open their eyes and their hearts and they will understand spiritual truth. Jesus called the Pharisees "blind leaders of the blind" (Matt. 15:14; 23:16–26). Satan is the prince of darkness (Luke 22:53) and he blinds the eyes of unbelievers (2 Cor. 4:1–6). As we witness to the lost, share the Scriptures with them, and pray for them, the Holy Spirit works to convict them and lead them to the Savior.

Sight: When You Trust Jesus, You Can See the Truth

I had been raised in Sunday school and church and had been confirmed in the church but had never been born again. Much seed had been planted in my heart, but it did not come to fruition until a few days short of my sixteenth birthday when I attended a Youth for Christ rally. That evening, as Billy Graham preached God's word, the Spirit convicted me and opened my eyes and my heart. I believed God's promise and accepted His Son as my Savior and Lord, and my life was radically changed. I could see!

To begin with, my eyes were opened to myself. I was a religious teenager but I was not a child of God. I needed to be born again. This does not mean that my pastors, Sunday school teachers, family, and friends had failed all those years, for they planted the seed and prayed for me and the seed bore fruit that night at the YFC rally. There my eyes were opened *to Jesus* and I received Him and became a child of God. My eyes were opened *to the Bible* and I had an insatiable appetite for reading and studying God's truth. I began to attend a Thursday evening Bible class and studied the epistle to the Hebrews. Pretty tough meat for a newborn Christian! But as I read and studied the Bible, my eyes were opened to *the will of God,* and I knew that the Lord wanted me in full-time ministry.

I thank the Lord for the adults that devoted time and energy to help ground me and the other new believers in the basics of the Christian life. They prayed for us, shared Christian books and magazines with us, and taught us the Scriptures week after week. During my years of ministry, it has been a joy to work with young believers and newly ordained pastors and encourage them in their walk and work. First Timothy 2:2 is still in the Bible and should be obeyed. All believers — young and old — must spend time daily in the Scriptures at home and also find a niche in a local church where they can worship and be taught and learn how to share the gospel with others.

Insight: As You Grow in Grace, You Can See Deeper

Insight is the ability to penetrate the inner nature of circumstances, people, concepts, and things. It is also the ability to grasp the hidden meaning of words, images, and teachings in the Bible. "Open my eyes, that I may see wondrous things from Your law" (Ps. 119:18) is a necessary prayer for every Bible student, along with "Turn away my eyes from looking at worthless things, and revive me in Your way" (119:37). The Danish Christian philosopher Søren Kierkegaard prayed, "Lord, give us weak eyes for things of little worth and eyes clear-sighted in all of your truth." Our teacher is the Holy Spirit (John 14:26), who enables us to compare Scripture with Scripture and discover new truths as we meditate on God's word, pray, and obey what God commands us to do. No sincere believer will carelessly scan the Bible but will take time to pause, pray, and ponder what the Lord has said. We should trace the cross references and let one passage shed light on other passages.

One of the marks of a maturing teacher of the word of God is his or her ability to let the Bible be its own commentator. Yes, we need teachers and commentaries, but we also need to take time to read the Bible carefully, check the cross-references, and meditate on God's truth. I recall the thrill I had as a young student discovering that Habakkuk 2:4 — "the just shall live by his faith" — is quoted three times in the New Testament: Romans 1:17, Galatians 3:11, and Hebrews 10:38. It is quoted at the beginning of Romans, where the major theme is "the just." You find it in the middle of Galatians, where the theme is how the just live. It is near the end of Hebrews, where the theme is "by faith." (See Hebrews 11, where "by faith" is found eighteen times.)

The tracing and studying of repeated biblical phrases is a wonderful way to discover the deeper truths of the Bible, so invest in a Bible with good cross references and buy a complete concordance to the version of the Bible that you study. I also urge you to secure a copy of *The New Treasury of Scripture Knowledge,* edited by Jerome H. Smith and published by Thomas Nelson. It is one Bible study tool I would not want to be without because it gives me thousands of cross references that help me better understand the verses I am studying.

Vision: We See the Invisible

If we could ask the believers we meet in the Bible and in church history, "How did you accomplish what you did?" they would probably reply, "The Lord gave us a vision, we trusted and obeyed, and He did the rest." Hebrews 11 makes it very clear that it was "by faith" that the heroes mentioned won their victories. The Lord gave Abraham and Sarah the vision of a mighty nation, starting with Isaac, their only son. Isaac shared the vision with Jacob, and God gave Jacob twelve sons who fathered the twelve tribes of Israel, God's people. Before Jacob died, he gave a special message to each of his sons (Gen. 49). Jacob's vision of God's calling sustained the Jewish people during centuries of suffering, and Joseph made them promise to bury him with his ancestors in the Promised Land (Gen. 50:22–26; Exod. 13:19). The Jewish patriarchs had a vision of a great nation dwelling in a great land, and God fulfilled every word of His covenant with His people.

God gave Moses the vision of a nation of pilgrims that would be delivered from Egypt and travel to the Promised Land, and by faith he led them out. Joshua had a vision of conquering the land, subduing its inhabitants, and establishing the nation of Israel; and the Lord honored his faith. After years of political and religious ups and downs, the nation became a kingdom under the leadership of David, ancestor of our Lord Jesus Christ, the "son of David." One of the most encouraging chapters in the Bible is 2 Samuel 7, God's covenant with David. Yes, David had his hours of temptation and defeat, but you find his name over a thousand times in the Bible and in the very first verse of the New Testament (Matt. 1:1). In fact, Jesus is called "the son of David."

Most if not all creative work done here on earth begins with vision. The artist "sees" the picture in his mind, makes a sketch to get him started, and a picture eventually is painted. The picture grows both in his mind and on the canvas. The architect imagines a building and draws what he sees in his mind, and soon you have blueprints. The composer hears the melody in his mind and sees the notes on the staff, jots them down, and has the beginning of a symphony. The author has a vision of some characters in a unique location involved in unusual circumstances, and he eventually writes a novel. The pastor meditates on a portion of Scripture and with the help of the Holy Spirit begins to "see" and "feel" a sermon. Whether it is cooking, decorating a room, preparing a speech, writing a poem, or planning a vacation, there is no way to avoid vision.

When Jesus wanted to focus the hearts of His disciples on evangelism, He said to them, "Behold, I say to you, lift up your eyes and look at the fields, for they are already white for harvest!" (John 4:35). Was He directing their vision toward the woman He had brought to salvation as she was bringing her friends from the city to the well? The apostles might have seen only Samaritan "enemies" coming, but Jesus saw a harvest of souls. Believers with keen spiritual vision see people, circumstances, and problems as God sees them, which simply means opportunity to bring blessing to needy people and glory to God. Sometimes we use the word "visionaries" to mean "dreamers," but in the Christian vocabulary, visionaries are "doers" and not "dreamers." If missionaries are not visionaries in the best sense, they will not accomplish much.

J. Hudson Taylor had a vision of taking the gospel to inland China, and that vision became the China Inland Mission. I recall the days when pastors and businessmen together envisioned a ministry to evangelize teenagers and servicemen, and Youth for Christ was born. Dwight L. Moody had a vision of building a school where people could study the Bible and be better prepared to serve in their local churches, and Moody Bible Institute was the result. Amy Carmichael's vision was to rescue the young girls in India from being kidnapped and forced into immorality and idolatry, and her ministry still goes on. God gave to Chuck Colson the vision to minister to men and women in prison and to their families back home, and Prison Fellowship is getting the job done.

First you receive the vision, then the vision grows as others join with you, and before you know it, the vision becomes an exciting reality that is ministering to people and glorifying the Lord.

The Lord saves sinners and moves them from blindness to sight. Then He moves His people from sight to insight, from insight to vision, and from vision to ministry reality. Like Moses, we see the invisible and eventually do the impossible! People tell us that it cannot be done, but the Bible and church history reply, "It has been done and will be done again!"

Will you be among the doers?

14

Losing What You Never Had

For the kingdom of heaven is like a man traveling to a far country, who called his own servants and delivered his goods to them. And to one he gave five talents, to another two, and to another one, to each according to his own ability; and immediately he went on a journey. Then he who had received the five talents went and traded with them, and made another five talents. And likewise he who had received two gained two more also. But he who had received one went and dug in the ground, and hid his lord's money. After a long time, the lord of those servants came and settled accounts with them. So he who had received five talents came and brought five other talents, saying, "Lord, you delivered to me five talents; look, I have gained five more talents besides them." His lord said to him, "Well done, good and faithful servant; you were faithful over a few things, I will make you ruler over many things. Enter into the joy of your lord." He also who had received two talents came and said, "Lord, you delivered to me two talents; look, I have gained two more talents besides them." His lord said to him, "Well done, good and faithful servant; you have been faithful over a few things, I will make you ruler over many things. Enter into the joy of your lord." Then he who had received the one talent came and said, "Lord, I know you to be a hard

> *man, reaping where you have not sown, and gathering where you have not scattered seed. And I was afraid, and went and hid your talent in the ground. Look, there you have what is yours." But his lord answered him and said to him, "You wicked and lazy servant, you knew that I reap where I have not sown, and gather where I have not scattered seed. Therefore you ought to have deposited my money with the bankers, and at my coming I would have received back my own with interest. Therefore take the talent from him, and give it to him who has ten talents. For to everyone who has, more will be given, and he will have abundance; but from him who does not have, even what he has will be taken away. And cast the unprofitable servant into the outer darkness. There will be weeping and gnashing of teeth." (Matt. 25:14–30)*

OUR LORD'S PARABLE of the talents could well be called "Don't fool yourself," or perhaps "The Christian life is serious, so give it your best." Here are three men, all serving the same master. The first two were rewarded with praise, promotion, and joy, while the third one lost everything and experienced loneliness, darkness, and pain.

But what does this have to do with God's people today? Read verse 13 and you will have the answer: "Watch therefore, for you know neither the day nor the hour in which the Son of Man is coming." When Jesus returns, God's people, alive on earth or buried in the earth, will be taken to heaven (1 Cor. 15:50–58; 1 Thess. 4:13–18) and we shall all stand before Him at His judgment seat and give an account of our works (Rom. 14:10–12; 2 Cor. 5:10). Those who have been faithful will receive rewards; the rest will be saved "yet as through fire" (1 Cor. 3:5–17). Each believer's faithfulness and service today will determine the rewards and assignments he or she will receive at the judgment seat of Christ.

This parable gives us some practical principles to grasp if we are to be prepared for our Lord's return and our appearing at His judgment seat.

Ability Leads to Opportunity

Today we use the word "talent" to describe the skills and abilities people are born with, but in New Testament times, a talent was a measure of money. It was equivalent to what the average day laborer could earn in one year. The master distributed the talents according to each servant's ability, so it was a fair assignment. The talents represent God-given opportunities to use one's abilities, and if the servant with one talent had earned another talent, he would have received the same reward as the other two servants.

It is not our fault if we lack the abilities that others possess. At our conception in the womb, our abilities were given to us and at our conversion we received our spiritual gifts (Ps. 139:13–16; 1 Cor. 12). My two older brothers were gifted with mechanical ability and athletic skill, while I lacked both. I have never been asked to repair a car or referee a sporting event. In fact, when I was in grade school, I was the last person chosen for every team. You and I must know our personal abilities and spiritual gifts, thank the Lord for them, and use them for doing His will and glorifying His name.

The third servant made the mistake of thinking that he was not important because he had only one talent and therefore very little ability. What can you do with so little? However, if he had invested that one talent and earned another one, he would have received his fair reward. The master knew that this servant was a wicked, lazy man (v. 26), yet he graciously gave him an opportunity to earn a promotion. "The real reward," wrote George Morrison, "is not the bigger task. It is the *capacity* to do the bigger task."[1] Christians who faithfully serve the Lord with a few things will grow in strength so that they can be rewarded with greater opportunities (vv. 21–23).

Young Joseph in prison was a faithful servant who ended up second ruler in Egypt (Gen. 39–41). David began as a shepherd boy and ultimately become Israel's greatest king. Ruth was a poor widow and an alien gleaner who loved and cared for her mother-in-law and married one of the wealthiest men in Bethlehem. She became an ancestress of Jesus. Joshua began as Moses' servant and became his successor and the conqueror of the Promised Land. Our Father does not want us to be lazy custodians, carefully protecting what He entrusts to us. He wants us to be faithful servants, workers, and investors who obey His will, grow strong, and become capable of doing bigger and better things. Cultivate the abilities and gifts you have been given, put them to work for the glory of the Lord, and He will develop you — and finally reward you.

Responsibility Involves Relationship

During the years I was a seminary student, before I was called to pastor a church, I held several part-time jobs with a variety of bosses. I soon learned how they related to the "big boss" and what was expected of them and of me, and I did my best to make my boss look good.

An employee who creates problems for his or her boss may end up searching for another job.

It's obvious that the third servant in our Lord's parable did not have a happy relationship with his master or his job. The servant's heart was not in his work or controlled by love for his master. He

---

1   George Morrison, *Highways of the Heart* (Grand Rapids: Kregel, 1994), 262.

saw the master as a demanding man who took all the credit for the work that other people performed (v. 24). The servant worked only when the master was watching — Paul called this "eyeservice" (Eph. 6:6; Col. 3:22) — and he probably felt humiliated for receiving only one talent. But his master was treating him fairly, for the servant did not have much ability or a great desire to work. His master was actually being very kind to him. Our personal relationship to our Lord is the key to a faithful and fruitful Christian life. He is the vine and we are the branches, and we must draw our strength from Him (John 15:1–8). Our Lord makes it very clear in John 15:5 that without Him we can do nothing.

No matter how much we have been trained or how experienced we may be in service, it is the blessing of God that makes our work fruitful. Unless we fellowship with Him daily in the word of God and prayer (Acts 6:4), we cannot know His will and do it for His glory. The third servant despised his master and cheated him out of the service owed to him. Instead of being rewarded, the servant was rebuked and rejected. I have known people who were angry with the Lord because He did not answer their prayers as they desired. They forgot Deuteronomy 6:5, "You shall love the LORD your God with all your heart, with all your soul, and with all your strength."

It is a privilege to serve the Lord and we should give Him our best. A servant's heart must be in his or her work or the work will become drudgery.

Stewardship Is Not Ownership

Not only did the third servant have the wrong attitude toward his master, but he also had a wrong attitude toward the talent the master had given him. He thought it was his and that he could do with it whatever he pleased. But we must remember that everything we possess — from our mind, body, and will (Rom. 12:1–2) to our dwelling and its furnishings, our financial resources, and even our daily schedule — all comes from the Lord and belongs to the Lord. We are stewards and must use what the Lord gives us to serve and honor Him. "The earth is the LORD's, and all its fullness, the world and those that dwell therein" (Ps. 24:1). "Moreover, it is required in stewards that one be found faithful" (1 Cor. 4:2).

The servant thought the talent was his so he buried it to protect it until the master claimed it, but he ended up giving it to the servant with the ten talents! "For to everyone who has, more will be given, and he will have abundance; but from him who does not have, even what he has will be taken away" (Matt. 25:29). The *Phillips Translation* reads, "Even his nothing will be taken away." There is a paradox for you! Several people in the Bible thought they had something but really had nothing, and their "nothing" was taken from them. Consider King Herod (Acts 12:20–23), Ananias and Sapphira (Acts 5:1–11), the rich young ruler (Mark 10:17–22), Queen Jezebel (2 Kings 9:30–37), Haman (Esther 5:11; 7:1–10), and Judas Iscariot (Acts 1:15–20). "For if anyone thinks himself to be something, when he is nothing, he deceives himself" (Gal. 6:3). What a contrast to our Lord Jesus Christ who became poor that we might become rich (2 Cor. 8:9).

Faith Conquers Fear and Leads to Obedience and Blessing

Because the unprofitable servant thought his master was a hard man to work for, he was controlled by fear and not faith (Matt. 25:24–25). He may have thought, "If I invest this money, suppose my investment fails or my talent is stolen? What will my master do to me?" Instead of being lazy on the job, if this careless servant had worked hard with the two other servants, he would have learned how to be successful. But now it was too late. What he wanted was protection, so he hid his single talent in the ground. He was afraid of his master and afraid of failure, yet he did everything he could to experience both. "The sluggard is wiser in his own eyes than seven men who can answer sensibly" (Prov. 26:16). Instead of admitting his own faults and changing his ways, the unprofitable servant blamed his master. It has well been said that the person who is good at excuses is rarely good at anything else.

Of itself, fear is not necessarily an enemy. Children must be taught to fear fire, heights, electric currents, poisons, sharp instruments, and the friendship of strangers. But fear that hides the face of God or turns us from prayer and the Scriptures is definitely an enemy. Fear paralyzes, but faith energizes.

The safest place in the world is in the will of God, for when we are in His will, we have no reason to be afraid. Like some people in the word of God, we may be crossing the Red Sea, or in a storm on the sea, or about to be thrown into a deadly fiery furnace. But if we are motivated by a love for our Master and are obedient to His will, we are safe and the Lord will see us through. "Behold, God is my salvation; I will not be afraid" (Isa. 12:2). "The LORD is my light and my salvation; whom shall I fear? The LORD is the strength of my life, of whom shall I be afraid?" (Ps. 27:1). "I sought the LORD, and He heard me, and delivered me from all my fears" (Ps. 34:4). "For God has not given us a spirit of fear, but of power and of love and of a sound mind" (2 Tim. 1:7).

There is work to be done before we meet the Lord, and He has equipped each of His children to do their part in the spread of the gospel.

Faith conquers fear and leads to obedience and blessing. "And this is the victory that has overcome the world — our faith" (1 John 5:4).

15

We Are Yoked to Be Free

Then He began to rebuke the cities in which most of His mighty works had been done, because they did not repent: "Woe to you, Chorazin! Woe to you, Bethsaida! For if the mighty works which had been done in you had been done in Tyre and Sidon, they would have repented long ago in sackcloth and ashes. But I say to you, it will be more tolerable for Tyre and Sidon in the day of judgment than for you. And you, Capernaum, who are exalted to heaven, will be brought down to Hades; for if the mighty works which were done in you had been done in Sodom, it would have remained until this day, But I say to you, it shall be more tolerable for the land of Sodom in the day of judgment than for you." At that time Jesus answered and said, "I thank You, Father, Lord of heaven and earth, because you have hidden these things from the wise and prudent and have revealed them to babes. Even so, Father, for so it seemed good in Your sight. All things have been delivered to Me by My Father, and no one knows the Son except the Father. Nor does anyone know the Father except the Son, and the one to whom the Son wills to reveal Him. Come to Me, all you who labor and are heavy laden, and I will give you rest. Take My

> yoke upon you and learn from Me, for I am gentle and lowly in
> heart, and you will find rest for your souls. For My yoke is easy
> and My burden is light." (Matt. 11:20–30)

WHEN HE WORKED with Joseph in the carpenter's shop, Jesus must have helped to build and repair yokes, for without yokes the farmers could not easily work their land. Throughout the Bible, wearing a yoke is a symbol of bondage (e.g., Deut. 28:48; Jer. 27; Gal. 5:1), while removing or breaking a yoke signifies freedom (e.g., Jer. 28:1–14). When Jewish boys attached themselves to a rabbi to study the law, they were said to have "taken his yoke."

The yoke that Jesus gives us leads us to freedom and not to bondage and helps us to grow in the Christian life. Unless we yield to Him, we cannot learn from Him and experience the blessings that He alone can give us. In Matthew 11:20–30, Jesus deals with three different kinds of people: the faithless (vv. 20–24), the helpless (vv. 25–27), and the restless (vv. 28–30).

Judgment: Jesus and the Faithless (11:20–24)

During His three years of public ministry, our Lord demonstrated His love for the people by traveling from place to place feeding the hungry, healing the afflicted and handicapped, delivering the demonized, and even raising the dead. His enemies said His power came from Satan (Matt. 12:22–30), but Peter had the right approach: "You are the Christ, the Son of God" (Matt. 16:16). Those who trusted Him entered into new life, but those who rejected Him forfeited eternal life. In this passage, the Lord indicts those who would not put their faith in Him. They had heard His messages and seen His miracles, yet they would not believe in Him and be saved. "But although He had done so many signs before them, they did not believe in Him" (John 12:37).

Capernaum was on the western shore of the Sea of Galilee, an important city in that day.

Jesus performed many miracles there, but the people chose not to believe in Him. Our Lord made Capernaum His headquarters ("home" in Mark 2:1) when He ministered in Galilee. Peter and Andrew came from Capernaum (Mark 1:21, 29). There was a synagogue in Capernaum and Peter's mother-in-law had her home in the city there and was healed by Jesus (Mark 1:29–31). Jesus performed many miracles in Capernaum: healing a demoniac (Mark 1:23–28) and a paralytic (Mark 2:1–12), raising Jairus' daughter from the dead, healing a woman with an issue of blood (Mark 5:21–43), and healing two blind men (Matt. 9:27–31) and a dumb demoniac (Mark 9:14–29). Chorazin and Bethsaida were important cities in their day, but, like Capernaum, they are no more.

There is certainly a challenge here for taking the gospel to cities and towns. Jesus did not ignore the people in these places, but neither did He pamper them. There came a day when their citizens had tested His longsuffering enough and He drew the line. While there are towns and cities in darkness today, in most places any sinner seeking salvation can turn on the radio or the TV and find a gospel program. Bibles are available even in grocery stores and drug stores, let alone most hotel rooms. There is enough gospel in some church advertisements to point the way to salvation. People today who are rejecting Jesus Christ are sinning against a flood of light. It is the task of the church to share the good news of salvation with a lost world and to pray that men and women, young people, and children will put their faith in Jesus.

Grace: Jesus and the Helpless (11:25–27)

Our Lord now speaks to His Father and thanks Him for His gracious love for the lost and His willingness to save the helpless "babes." The religious leaders in Jesus' day were proud of their knowledge of the Scriptures, their beautiful temple in Jerusalem, and their faithfulness to meet weekly in the synagogues. The priests, scribes, and Pharisees were "wise and prudent" and yet they did not recognize their own Messiah but had the Son of God arrested and crucified! If they had humbled themselves and become as helpless as babes He would have saved them. It is not the proud achievers that God saves but the humble babes who know they cannot save themselves:

> For you see your calling, brethren, that not many wise according to the flesh, not many mighty, not many noble, are called. But God has chosen the foolish things of the world to put to shame the wise, and God has chosen the weak things of the world to put to shame the things which are mighty; and the base things of the world and the things which are despised God has chosen, and the things that are not, that no flesh should glory in His presence. (1 Cor. 1:26–29)

Have you classified yourself as a helpless sinful babe, or are you trying to impress the Father with your conduct and character?

God the Son reveals the Father to us. "He who has seen Me has seen the Father," Jesus told His disciples (John 14:9). What Jesus says and does as recorded in the Bible shows us the person and work of the Father. When we read that Jesus took the children in His arms, we see the Father loving the little ones. When Jesus forgave sinners we see the Father, the Lord of heaven and earth, forgiving them and taking them into His family. The Father has given all things to His Son (v. 27), and the Son makes all things available to those who have been born again. "He who did not spare His own Son, but delivered Him up for us all, how shall He not with Him freely give us all things?" (Rom. 8:32). Whatever we need we may ask for and "my God shall supply all your need according to His riches in glory by Christ Jesus" (Phil. 4:19). "The Father loves the Son, and has given all things into His hand" (John 3:35; see John 13:3).

Peace: Jesus and the Restless (11:28–30)

We come now to our paradox: wearing the yoke Christ gives you enables you to find rest and freedom in your heart. We are yoked that we might be free! The British theologian P. T. Forsyth wrote, "The first duty of every soul is to find not its freedom but its Master."[1] I live in a city with a university that is recognized for developing excellent football teams. How does a student achieve greatness in a sport? By putting himself or herself under the tutelage of a great coach. Submission is the way to success. Our university also has a fine school of music. How do students become first-rate musicians? By putting themselves under the guidance and discipline of gifted instructors and exchanging freedom for discipline and growth. Then one day they have the freedom to perform skillfully because they found the right masters. The way to freedom is obedience to the right master, and for Christians, that master is Jesus Christ, the Son of God.

Moses gave the people of Israel a rule about yokes that teaches us an important spiritual principle: "You shall not plow with an ox and a donkey together" (Deut. 22:10). The reason is obvious: the two animals are radically different and would find it difficult to work together. The apostle Paul used this rule to teach the Corinthian believers not to be yoked with unbelievers (2 Cor. 6:11–18). In the Jewish law, the donkey was an unclean animal, while the

---

1   P. T. Forsyth, *Positive Preaching and the Modern Mind* (Grand Rapids: Baker), 28. See also p. 71.

ox was a clean animal. The donkey is impulsive and independent, while the ox is slow and deliberate. During my pastoral years, I saw the unequal yoke bring pain and sorrow to marriages and business partnerships.

We live in a restless world. We can travel and communicate faster and better today than ever before, but sometimes we pay a price for these privileges. How often discerning physicians give to troubled patients a prescription of two words: "Slow down!" Life was much simpler in Jesus' day and you would think that everybody would have a calm heart. But here is the Master inviting the crowd to discover the healing medicine of a restful heart! St. Augustine was correct when he wrote, "Thou hast made us for Thyself, and our hearts are restless until they rest in Thee." We can go to the pharmacy and purchase sleep, but we cannot purchase rest and peace. Our Lord gives us four instructions that, if obeyed, will quiet the restless troubled heart.

Come. To come to Christ means to submit to Him and trust Him as Savior and Lord. We cannot come to the founders of the so-called great religions because these men and women are dead and can do nothing for us. But Jesus is alive and able to help us, no matter how desperate the situation may be. The patient in the hospital, the prisoner in the jail, the mechanic under the automobile, the child on the playground can all turn to Jesus right where they are and He will save them. "And it shall come to past that whoever calls on the name of the LORD shall be saved" (Acts 2:21, quoting Joel 2:32). The evening I was saved I was standing against the back wall of a high school auditorium, serving as an usher and listening to Billy Graham speak. While he was speaking, I lifted my heart to Jesus and trusted Him, and He saved me! I did not go forward and I was not counseled, *but I was saved!* I simply came by faith to Jesus and He received me.

The word "come" implies that lost sinners are heading in the wrong direction, following the wrong crowd, and doing the wrong things. They must turn around, go to Christ, and follow Him. He is all we need and there is no reason to look elsewhere. No matter the circumstances, we may turn around, trust Jesus, and start following Him. Come as you are and receive Him as He is, leaving all your sinful baggage at the cross where Jesus bore our sins (1 Peter 2:24). If you are carrying a heavy burden and laboring to get rid of it, your works will never save you. We are saved "not by works of righteousness which we have done, but according to His mercy He saved us" (Titus 3:5).

Take. Our Lord does not force His yoke upon us; He wants us to accept it willingly and wear it joyfully. Why? Because this will take us deeper into our relationship with Him. When we come to Jesus by faith, we are given peace *with* God (Rom. 5:1); and when we take His yoke and wear it, we are given the peace *of* God (Phil. 4:6–7). Peace *with* God means that our sins are forgiven and we have a right standing before God. We are members of God's family and will be for eternity. The peace *of* God is the quiet confidence we have that God is in control and we have nothing to fear. Peace *with* God means we are saved; the peace *of* God means we are safe.

What does Jesus mean by "taking His yoke"? It means accepting the will of God and obeying it. God has a perfect plan for each of His children, and when we obey that plan, we please the Father, glorify the Son, and enjoy the ministry of the Holy Spirit in our lives. I have met believers who have had the erroneous idea that the will of God is difficult to discover and dangerous to obey, that it takes all the joy out of the Christian life. How foolish! Remember, "The counsel of the LORD stands forever, the plans of His heart to all generations" (Ps. 33:11). How can the will of God be difficult to discover and dangerous to obey *when that will comes from God's loving heart and is designed personally for each believer?* Generally speaking, there are commands and warnings in Scripture that all believers must obey, but God also speaks to us specifically as we ponder the word of God and pray to know His will. No one has the same life plan; each of God's children is an original. The yoke of sin is a heavy burden (Ps. 38:4) and so is the yoke of religion (Matt. 23:4; Acts 15:10). But the yoke of Christ is easy and the burden is light — and Christ bears the yoke with us! What more could we want?

Learn. If we want to grow in grace and become more like the Master, we must grow in our knowledge of the Master. "But grow in the grace and knowledge of our Lord and Savior Jesus Christ" (2 Peter 3:18). We come to Him by faith and He becomes our savior. We take His yoke and He becomes our master. And now we learn from Him and He becomes our teacher and our example.

This does not mean simply buying some textbooks and studying the Bible with their help, as important as that may be. Even unsaved people can do that. It means using every tool that we have as we study the word of God daily, meditate on it, and experience the transforming power of God's truth. "And you shall know the truth, and the truth shall make you free" (John 8:32). Our Lord spent three years teaching His disciples so they could take over the ministry on earth when He returned to heaven, and they in turn taught others. Three of them wrote inspired biographies of Jesus and others wrote inspired letters about the person, work, and teachings of our Lord. The Old Testament gives us the historical and prophetic background of New Testament events and should also be read and studied. "The New is in the Old concealed; the Old is by the New revealed."

It is important that we get to know Jesus Christ better as we learn from the Bible privately and hear it read and expounded publicly. This not only builds us up personally, but it gives us the enlightenment and nourishment we need to live a godly life and be able to minister to others. The word of God is like a mirror in which we see both ourselves and the glory of God. By beholding God's glory in the word, we are transformed by the Holy Spirit to become more and more like Jesus (James 1:21–25; 2 Cor. 3:18). As the old hymn expresses it, we must "take time to be holy." We live in an "information age" and must not allow shallow conversations and entertainment and useless reading to rob us of the time we must spend with the Lord.

Find rest. When you come to Christ in faith, He gives you rest; and when you take His yoke and learn about Him, He helps you find rest for your soul, heart, mind, and conscience. It is "the peace of God which surpasses all understanding" (Phil. 4:7). In the upper room Jesus told His disciples, "Peace I leave with you, My peace I give to you; not as the world gives do I give to you. Let not your heart be troubled, neither let it be afraid" (John 14:27). In Jesus' day, the Roman world was arrogant and brutal, but our Lord was gentle and lowly in heart — *and He still is!* Though occasionally He might seem to hurt us, He will never harm us. Hurting becomes healing when the Savior chastens us and then applies the medicine of His grace (Heb. 12:1–11). The world tries to give peace by distraction, entertainment, or even sedation, but these temporary placebos rarely bring lasting peace.

As a father or mother calms a frightened child, so our loving heavenly Father calms His children:

> The LORD your God in your midst, the Mighty One, will save;
> He will rejoice over you with gladness, He will quiet you in His
> love, He will rejoice over you with singing. (Zeph. 3:17)

This is a picture of our heavenly Father holding His frightened children on His lap and singing to them! We know that the Lord Jesus sang when here on earth (Matt. 26:30) and that the Holy Spirit sings through the church at worship (Eph. 5:18–21), but the prophet tells us that the Father also sings! If we yield ourselves to the Father, He will take us in His arms and sing us into rest. I can assure you that you can trust this promise.

We cannot control the weather, the people and circumstances around us, or the disturbing news we read, hear, or see. We cannot always manage how we feel. But we can control how we handle all of this. As children of the heavenly Father who dearly loves us, we can respond to His Son's invitation and experience peace in the midst of distress, disappointment, and suffering. Jesus says, "Come, take My yoke; learn of Me and find rest."

We are yoked that we might be freed. Jesus does not give us peace in place of trial but *peace in the midst of trial!* He uses the trials to mature us, not to harm us.

"Come to Me — and I will give you rest."